Astrological Keywords
Signs of the Zodiac

Fundamental and Traditional Astrological Key
Ideas about the Signs of the Zodiac

Michael Munkasey
© 2022

Copyright © 2022 by Michael Munkasey
Southern California, USA

All Rights Reserved

Without limiting the rights reserved above under copyright, no part of this publication may be reproduced, stored in, or introduced into a retrieval system, or transmitted in any form or by any means (electronic, mechanical, photocopying, scanning, recording or otherwise), without written permission from both the author and the publisher, except in the case of brief quotations embodied in reviews and articles.

The scanning, uploading and distribution of this book via the Internet, or via any other means, without the written permission of the publisher is illegal and punishable by law. Please do not encourage electronic Cover

Requests and inquires may be mailed to:

American Federation of Astrologers (AFA)
6553 S. Rural Road
Tempe, AZ 85283, USA

Cover background art: Nasa images: Tadpole Nebula, Image Credit: Juan Ignacio Jimenez, https://creativecommons.org/licenses/by/4.0/

Cover design: Celeste Nash-Weninger

ISBN: 978-0-86690-680-7

Published by: The American Federation of Astrologers (AFA), Tempe, AZ

www.astrologers.com

This book is dedicated to all astrological students, practitioners and teachers who desire to expand their insights, understanding and practice.

Table of Contents

Foreword	v
Introduction	vi
Chapter 1: From Symbols to Words	1
Chapter 2: The Signs	9

Sign Keyword References

Aries — 13

Aries Adjective Essence	13
18 Aries Adjective Themes Grouped	14
66 Aries Adjective Keywords Alphabetically	15
Aries Noun Essence	17
13 Aries Noun Themes Grouped	18
51 Aries Noun Keywords Alphabetically	19

Taurus — 21

Taurus Adjective Essence	21
23 Taurus Adjective Themes Grouped	22
82 Taurus Adjective Keywords Alphabetically	24
Taurus Noun Essence	26
18 Taurus Noun Themes Grouped	27
65 Taurus Noun Keywords Alphabetically	28

Gemini — 31

Gemini Adjective Essence	31
16 Gemini Adjective Themes Grouped	32

60 Gemini Adjective Keywords Alphabetically — 33
Gemini Noun Essence — 35
12 Gemini Noun Themes Grouped — 36
46 Gemini Noun Keywords Alphabetically — 37

Cancer — 39
Cancer Adjective Essence — 39
26 Cancer Adjective Themes Grouped — 40
98 Cancer Adjective Keywords Alphabetically — 42
Cancer Noun Essence — 44
27 Cancer Noun Themes Grouped — 45
105 Cancer Noun Keywords Alphabetically — 47

Leo — 49
Leo Adjective Essence — 49
16 Leo Adjective Themes Grouped — 50
59 Leo Adjective Keywords Alphabetically — 51
Leo Noun Essence — 53
14 Leo Noun Themes Grouped — 54
55 Leo Noun Keywords Alphabetically — 55

Virgo — 57
Virgo Adjective Essence — 57
22 Virgo Adjective Themes Grouped — 58
83 Virgo Adjective Keywords Alphabetically — 60
Virgo Noun Essence — 62
23 Virgo Noun Themes Grouped — 63
79 Virgo Noun Keywords Alphabetically — 64

Libra	**67**
Libra Adjective Essence	67
26 Libra Adjective Themes Grouped	68
97 Libra Adjective Keywords Alphabetically	70
Libra Noun Essence	72
24 Libra Noun Themes Grouped	73
80 Libra Noun Keywords Alphabetically	75
Scorpio	**77**
Scorpio Adjective Essence	77
20 Scorpio Adjective Themes Grouped	78
79 Scorpio Adjective Keywords Alphabetically	80
Scorpio Noun Essence	82
14 Scorpio Noun Themes Grouped	83
56 Scorpio Noun Keywords Alphabetically	84
Sagittarius	**87**
Sagittarius Adjective Essence	87
21 Sagittarius Adjective Themes Grouped	88
80 Sagittarius Adjective Keywords Alphabetically	90
Sagittarius Noun Essence	92
15 Sagittarius Noun Themes Grouped	93
57 Sagittarius Noun Keywords Alphabetically	94
Capricorn	**97**
Capricorn Adjective Essence	97
22 Capricorn Adjective Themes Grouped	98
81 Capricorn Adjective Keywords Alphabetically	99

Capricorn Noun Essence	101
14 Capricorn Noun Themes Grouped	102
55 Capricorn Noun Keywords Alphabetically	103
Aquarius	**105**
Aquarius Adjective Essence	105
17 Aquarius Adjective Themes Grouped	106
67 Aquarius Adjective Keywords Alphabetically	107
Aquarius Noun Essence	109
19 Aquarius Noun Themes Grouped	110
75 Aquarius Noun Keywords Alphabetically	112
Pisces	**115**
Pisces Adjective Essence	115
21 Pisces Adjective Themes Grouped	116
84 Pisces Adjective Keywords Alphabetically	118
Pisces Noun Essence	120
18 Pisces Noun Themes Grouped	121
71 Pisces Noun Keywords Alphabetically	122
The Overall Alphabetical list	125
References and Sources	159

Foreword

by: Adam Gainsberg

Many astrologers know instinctively that our beloved astrology is a language. But Michael Munkasey has spent decades proving it… pouring through hundreds of thousands of words in the English language. What an effort!

Be forewarned… this book will overturn your opinion that astrological keywords are quickly consumed at best, or trite and dumbed-down at worst. Longtime astrologer and researcher Michael Munkasey has spent literal years grouping the entire contents of both the thesaurus and dictionary to arrive at what you hold in your hand – an exhaustive compilation of keywords and themes for each of astrology's twelve signs.

Thanks to his enduring passion for both the meaning and the meaning overlap of words, we now have an invaluable resource for accurately distilling the essence of each astrological sign into a complete set of keywords readily available and pragmatically useful for every type of astrologer under the Sun…equally. This is the essential power of what Michael has produced. In exploiting the most basic building block of language itself – words, he's created a kind of re-engineered "All Are Welcome" permanent invitation to share the astrological language across traditions and techniques.

Each sign is first essentialized into its noun essence and its adjective essence, consistent with Michael's fundamental premise that astrology is first and foremost a language unto itself. Each essence paragraph is then followed by grouped sets of keyword themes along with the full list of the alphabetized keywords used in the theme groupings.

The educational possibilities here are blatant. Michael's system of languaging the signs into keywords, key phrases and themes will do more for current and future astrological students than words can convey. And astrological professionals would do equally well to use the invaluable lists he provides as both review and invitation to create their own lists of sign-as-noun and sign-as-adjective.

As an astrological educator, it is difficult to resist the prediction that any future astrologer or astrolyte will, quite simply, be better at their chosen specialty having utilized this system of sign meanings in the celestial language we all share.

Adam Gainsburg
Founder, SoulsignAstrology.com

Introduction

Keywords are an important part of astrology. Keywords provide the common words needed to convert astrological symbols into everyday meaning. You see the astrological symbol for Virgo, or Aquarius, etc., but what do those symbols mean in everyday language? What are meaningful and insightful Virgo, Aquarius, etc., keywords?

The astrological keywords and key ideas presented in my works give you an in-depth sign, planet, etc., vocabulary. This book, with just the sign keywords, continues on from my 2018 book "House Keywords and More …". Other books on keywords for the planets, aspects, etc., may follow on. The House keywords book contains a more thorough introduction to keyword and rulership theory in general and you should refer to it for important back¬ground information.

The terms "keywords" and "key ideas" are similar, except that "keyword" implies a single word, while "key ideas" can include more than one word. An Aries keyword is "advancing", while an Aries key idea is "moving forward". As used in these books the term "keyword" also includes and implies the term "key idea".

Keywords are not rulerships. Rulerships are an important ancient carry-over about strong affiliations of certain planets with signs of the zodiac. Keywords are words, language, used to describe the essence of the signs and planets. Often the terms 'keywords' and 'rulerships' are used interchange¬ably, but they are different. Planetary rulerships of signs follow an orderly arrangement and carry an importance of their own.

Nor are keywords astrological delineations. Delineation is an explanation of multiple astrological symbols considered together. This is done using keywords. But without access to meaningful and accurate keywords a good delineation is difficult to come by. Learn to use keywords well and your understanding and practice of astrology will greatly improve.

Michael Munkasey
Southern California, USA

Chapter One

From Symbols to Words

What are Astrological Keywords?

Keywords show word correlations between astrological symbols and language. For thousands of years words have been consistently used to describe the astrological parts. The words to describe, say, the zodiacal sign of Gemini, in the Greek, Egyptian, Medieval, and such earlier empires, are pretty much the same today as they were then. This book presents the core of those word ideas with a modern orientation.

The seven parts of astrology are: planets (this includes asteroids, dwarf planets, bodies beyond Pluto, etc.), signs, aspects, personal points (the Ascendant, MC, Vertex, etc.), houses, fixed stars, and long precessional cycles (based on the estimated 25,920 year precessional cycle). Each of these "parts" has an energy associated with it that can be described in words (language).

Popularly, only five of these parts are used in daily astrological work: planets, signs, chart angles, houses and aspects. I prefer to call the chart angles the Personal Sensitive Points (PSPs). There are seven of these parts that fall out from the combination of time, space and location that form the basis of the astrological diagram. When the orbit of the Earth's Moon is included with this astronomical chart diagram, then the Moon's Node becomes an eighth PSP.

Astrology as a Language

Language is in constant change. Over short and long periods of time both spoken and written language evolve, change and adapt.

In this book I introduce new concepts, and this is based on the observation that, in one sense, <u>Astrology is a Language</u>. Astrology starts with symbols, usually placed in a diagram called a chart, and then words (language) are used by an astrologer to describe the placements, effects and interchanges of those symbols within that diagram.

There is a direct correlation between language words and the corresponding astrological symbols. This book presents a modern equating of the Symbols of Astrology to the Language of 21st century American English.

American English as an example has nouns, adjectives, verbs, etc., as its parts of speech. Astrology has planets, signs, aspects, etc., as its parts of expression.

Important Concept: there is a one-to-one correlation between the parts of language and astrology's parts!

Planets can be interpreted by using the noun, adjective or adverb words of language. Signs can be represented by noun or adjective words. The PSPs use the same parts of speech as the planets. Houses also use nouns, but only the "noun things", as opposed to the "noun qualities" used by the planets and PSPs. Aspects associate with the verbs.

When assigning a word to its astrological part it is important to note the word's part of speech (noun, adjective, etc.). Adverbs in most instances are adjectives with the end "ly" affixed. Example: quiet (adjective), and quietly (adverb).

Example 1: The zodiacal sign of Gemini associates with the Third House. But the sign of Gemini is <u>not</u> the Third House. Sample Third House "noun thing" keywords include: siblings, transportation, early schooling, etc. Sample Gemini "noun" keywords include: adaptability, explanation, likeness, conversation, etc.

Example 2: "Saturn in Aries" can be expressed by Saturn adjectives, and Aries noun combinations. I call such combinations "frases".

One traditional adjective keyword for Saturn is "cautious", and a noun keyword for Aries is "forward movement". This combination for Saturn in Aries becomes "cautious forward movement", or, "moves forward cautiously", or "proceeds cautiously". Use the variety presented in this book to your advantage. Of course that is only one frase, but without having a thorough keyword reference for the planets, signs, etc., then where can you find a comprehensive set of astrological keywords for chart interpretations?

Here! In this book!

Arranging Words into Themes

This is an original work. Years of thought and effort on my part have gone into accumulating words and then classifying those into a usable arrangement. It is their arrangement, essence, which became important.

Acquiring words that associate with the parts of astrology is relatively easy. First you study astrology for many years to learn about the core meaning of its symbols. You then begin to realize that everyday words associate with those symbols. Then you start to collect words and make word assignments for the astrological planets, signs, etc. Before long you can accumulate hundreds and hundreds, even thousands, of words. I used a thesaurus to assist with gathering words, but everyday news events, interactions with people, etc., also contributed words to my compiling.

How did I do this? I read through a thesaurus and also a dictionary entry by entry, noting each entry's part of speech, and then assigning the word to its appropriate place. Eventually I accumulated over 20,000 house words, and over 60,000 planet, sign, aspect, etc., words.

If I encountered a noun entry and it was a noun "thing" then I assigned that word to a house. If I encountered a noun and it was a noun quality, then I assigned it to a planet or sign. For example: noun "thing" words include: pencil, flowers, dishes, desk, etc. Noun quality words include: precision, praise, authorization, involvement, etc. I used a computer data base program to manage these words. The time it took to sort through 60,000 or more words was just a few seconds.

The accumulated words may start out as (say) Leo words. Put them into a Leo holding 'bucket' according to their part of speech (noun or adjective for a sign). These buckets, in this example, the Leo noun bucket or the Leo adjective bucket, are used to hold accumulated words by their part of speech. Soon you notice that those many words in a particular bucket fall into just a few significant categories, or themes, or groupings – where one theme category described in three or four words can represent many, many of the accumulated word ideas.

The time consuming work involves taking the many words gathered in general, for example, the over 600 words accumulated in the Leo adjective bucket, and then extracting from those accumulated words the important categories or themes that represent the astrological part, like Leo adjective. You look through the words related to a planet or sign and then try to place those into an appropriate category or theme. This reduces the many gathered words into a reasonable number of theme ideas. And it is those theme ideas that represent the essence of the planet, sign, etc.

The implication is that I have not copied from others their word to astrological part assignments. I have tried very hard to mirror accepted astrological tradition in my word base, but what I have produced is new and unique. The themes I have extracted are shown in this book. It has taken many years of effort, but viable results are now available. How long did it take me to comb through and assign (say) 600 Leo adjectives into their related themes? Weeks and weeks. Then more time and effort to ensure there was minimal overlap of theme ideas among the categories.

Language is plastic - that is, it stretches, changes with the needs of the user, etc. A word can have one meaning today, and then another meaning added tomorrow or the next day. A word can mean one thing to person A and another thing to person B.

Individual words can also take on many different meanings.

Example: take the word "hard", and its variations. There is: hard and fast, hard-boiled, hard to say, hard time, hard at it, hard to believe, too hard to do, etc. The word 'hard' can be used to represent the ideas: firm and solid; or, puzzling; or, unbearable; or, laborious, etc. When words have multiple different meanings they overlap with astrological symbols. Thus you can associate the word "hard" with Taurus, in one sense, Saturn in another sense, Mercury in another sense, and so forth.

Keywords vs. Delineation

This is a reference book about keywords. <u>Keywords are not delineations</u>. A delineation is an explanation of an astrological energy (i.e., symbol) combination that carries meaning and insight for a user, client or application. But to get to a delineation you need a good and well-presented keyword compendium. Much effort was made to obtain and extract those themes, but eventually that effort became this book.

My 2018 AFA Publishers (Arizona, USA) near 400-page book "House Keywords and More …" contains over 14,000 House keywords. These are broken down into eighteen categories, by House. Category examples include: horary word associations, things relating the house, members of the family, afflictions, colors, etc. Its opening chapters also explain my views of how keywords work. This series of books follows on from that work and is addresses the Planets, Signs, Aspects and PSPs. These books work together covering different astrological areas and each is needed.

This book presents astrological zodiacal theme word ideas (i.e., keywords) two ways: by theme category, and alphabetically within a topic (like a sign or planet). Subsequent books will present planet, etc., themes.

Within each sign, planet, etc., there is a grouping for the relevant part of speech. E.g., Aries Nouns, Moon Adjectives, Midheaven Nouns. Note as you examine these categories how different the words are between the noun and adjective sets.

The most important part of this book is the theme categories. The theme categories shown in this book are presented in NO Special Order – each theme grouping is important. Each theme group carries an idea thrust that is related. The themes group together around a central idea that can be best expressed within a series of a few words.

When you look at, say, Libra Nouns, you can see I have identified 24 distinct and different energy theme groups within the over 600 Libra's noun words I had accumulated over many years. Libra, the zodiacal sign, is but one astrological energy essence. When the body of words accumulated (e.g., Libra Nouns) is broken into distinct categories, called themes, you can see the essence, or basic nature of the sign, planet, etc.

Memorizing just a few central keywords in a theme and using those exclusively does not bring on a well-rounded approach. A proficient person will study and retain a large number of keywords for each category, and then practice using those as circumstances warrant. Flexibility and the use of a large number of keywords can improve your overall astrological abilities by bringing out shades of meaning that may otherwise remain hidden.

Examples of Usage

Example 1: under the Taurus Adjective theme groupings you can find this set: *Patient (long-suffering), Enduring (long-lasting), and Tolerant (patient).*

These three theme words convey the Taurus-related key idea (thrust) of having patience and maintaining tolerance through time.

Example 2: under the Leo Adjective theme groupings you can find this set: *Dignified (distinguished), Imposing (dignified), Noble (distinguished), and Aristocratic (dignified).*

These four theme words convey the Leo-related key idea (thrust) of exhibiting a noble and distinguished bearing, a dignified look.

As a user you should do your own evaluation of the presented theme groups. The sign or planet essence, in the words of everyday language, lies within those word and energy groups for the sign, planet, aspect, etc.

For instance, over time I had accumulated some 776 Libra Adjective words, and extracted from those 776 words 26 important and identifiable "Theme Groups" from them.

What to do when you want to know more about Libra? The Libra Noun groups present ideas like: the process of agreement; the process of partnership, the process of having choices, the process of determining legality, etc. There are 24 such Libra Noun categories. Theme groupings for the signs, etc., are presented for you in this book.

The Alphabetical Index of All

There is also an alphabetical index of all 1731 themes included.

Overlaps

You may see that there are overlaps of the same word themes between and among the signs and planets, etc. There is no way to avoid that as the overlapping seems to fall out from the astrological energy associations and the way words are used in language and communication. The overlapping is good, in a sense, because then the energies can be expressed in more than one way, as opposed to just having one outlet.

The theme idea of sturdiness, something that lasts, being able to continue through time, having a duration, etc., lies with Saturn primarily. But it is also present in energies associated with Taurus.

There are Rulerships, and there are also Affinities. Example: Movement (activity) has association both as an Aries word and also a Mercury word. The Aries connotation is motion in a forward direction, while the Mercury usage connotation has a nervousness movement thrust. Many such overlaps exist.

In order to work well with keywords you need to understand sign and house rulerships by the planets. Please refer to my "House Keywords Book and More …", for an explanation of this relationship, or, see a short explanation in the section that follows.

A Final Note

One possible use of these Sign keywords can be in applying them to the Houses of a chart. If the sign on the Third House cusp of your chart is, say, Leo, then you can use the Leo adjective and noun themes to add more insightful shades of meaning to this House's interpretation.

In this book a sign heading will state: "xxx Theme Words … were compiled from a Base of about yyy Words … ". What that means is xxx theme words were extracted from the body of this sign or body's (total number) of about yyy words. Why is the word "about" there? Because I am still adding and moving words around. The data is a moving target.

Please realize that it is the theme groupings, the accumulation of central sign ideas, and not the write-ups, which accompany each sign, that are the central and most important part of this work. Focus on the themes.

There is a lot of information in this book. Take some time to read through the themes presented here, to see how they seem to hang together, to see how they do keep a relationship to their central sign energy. Realize that each individual sign can present a wide variety of meaning. Focusing on just a few of the theme groupings does not make for a well-rounded approach.

One exercise you may want to do to help expand your insight is to take a chart and interpret a portion of that chart with the sign keywords you presently know. Make a record of those thoughts by writing them down. Then take the same chart section and re-interpret it using a different set of theme keywords. Each version presents one view of reality. Each such exercise helps you to become a more well rounded person.

Chapter Two

The Signs

There is an ancient astrological tradition that defines twelve signs of the zodiac. According so some learned academics, this tradition goes back perhaps well over 12,000 years. According to some modern "scientists" this tradition is incorrect – but then what do these people, unschooled in astrology and its nature, know? They know only enough to sow confusion.

The signs do not initiate actions. That is the role of the planets. The signs provide energies, concepts, that modify and help shape the planet, PSP, house cusp, etc., meanings. You should try to take the theme meanings for the signs presented in this work and apply them to your House cusps, your PSPs, your planets, etc., to provide new insights and meanings.

Important Concept: The twelve signs of the zodiac, going from Aries to Pisces, each have a dual rulership – that is a yang ruler, and a yin ruler. This DUAL rulership concept is very important to recognize and use.

To understand this dual rulership schema I introduce two little-recognized Bodies that Work as Planets. I call them Psyche and Vulcan. They are not asteroids, they are planetary bodies. Over 35 years of investigation has not disappointed me as to their rulership importance.

Here is the dual rulership scheme the zodiacal signs. This scheme is explained more fully in my book "House Keywords and More …". Please also refer to that book.

SIGN	YANG RULER	YIN RULER
Aries	Mars	Pluto
Taurus	Venus	Psyche
Gemini	Mercury	Vulcan
Cancer	Moon	Sun
Leo	Sun	Moon
Virgo	Vulcan	Mercury
Libra	Psyche	Venus
Scorpio	Pluto	Mars
Sagittarius	Neptune	Jupiter
Capricorn	Uranus	Saturn
Aquarius	Saturn	Uranus
Pisces	Jupiter	Neptune

This is NOT a random arrangement of planets and signs! Notice that with the inclusion of the planet bodies Psyche and Vulcan both of the "Ruler" columns remain in a distinct and consistent planetary order, one going from down to up, and the other going from an up to down order.

Look at how the order of the planet bodies from inner to outer order is not broken. It remains consistent in both columns.

Next, notice that the planetary pairings remain consistent. Mars is with Pluto, Mercury is with Vulcan, The Sun is with the Moon, etc.

Next notice that the ancient rulership scheme (that used before the modern application of Uranus, Neptune and Pluto) remains preserved.

Next, notice that the consistent pairings are in three aspect orders: quincunx (Mars-Pluto, Venus-Psyche), square (Mercury-Vulcan, Jupiter-Neptune), and semi-sextile (Sun-Moon, Saturn-Uranus).

There is an intelligent order to this arrangement and approach. The solidity and consistency within the columns shout for recognition.

Please refer to the Psyche article I wrote for in the 1993 Llewellyn anthology, Noel Tyl, Editor, "Exploring Consciousness in the Horoscope".

Please refer to the article on Vulcan by Lynn Koiner in the 1993 Llewellyn anthology, Noel Tyl, Editor, "Astrology's Special Measurements".

The Planets remain as the source for astrological energies, and the Signs lend shadings and variations to those energies.

Essences of the Signs

Reminder: Keywords and their themes are not delineations. But you need a good keyword base to obtain astrological delineations, i.e., explanations and interpretations that are needed in astrological practices. Following, in an abbreviated paragraph form, are the essences (i.e., themes) of the signs from their adjective and noun perspectives.

The following presents keyword highlights. These are like snapshots or overviews, not total insights. People or events are not "pure" in their sign representations. When forming a delineation you need to take the whole chart pattern into consideration. Delineations require a good keyword base.

12   The Signs

Aries

Rulers: Yang Mars and Yin Pluto

Aries (Adjective) **Essence**

The Aries adjective thrust shows a focus on beginning, starting, approaching, appointing and moving forward. There can also be a rushing into circumstances, often with impulsiveness. This brings an eagerness that can arouse and excite. It is helped by a positive and determined intention backed by energy. This may lead to dogmatic and opinionated outlooks, many even brusque and inconsiderate. Areas that tend to be dry, smelly or dirty are associated with Aries adjectives.

Aries adjectives focus on a positive outlook; a certainty; and a need to move forward that permeates their intentions. An interest in setting an approach, producing expectations, defining the form of an early arrival, and controlling the start of action can also be found here. Their ardent, even pushy, energy, their thrust for a positive start, and a need to control the introduction of ongoing events is also a part of the Aries adjective quality.

Aries adjectives are content with the new, the pristine, the unmarked; and this need for a fresh approach shows much of their inner nature. They know how to provide emphasis and be insistent about their intentions and approaches. If there is something to be named, a first opportunity, or a start of something being established, then there is usually an Aries adjective input contributing to this forward momentum.

Aries adjectives portray a pushiness, impulsiveness and exhibit a tendency to not think matters through. Aries adjectives are content to let matters develop as is, even when there has been a lack of forethought about potential futures. This may be due to a dogmatic and self-convincing bent. Aries adjectives harbor a curtness, brusqueness and even rudeness if interrupted. Aries adjectives show a need for being considered first.

Aries adjectives bring an arrogance that covers their way of thinking. The "It is my way or the highway" idea remains foremost. There can be self-centeredness, and the idea that opinions and presumptions should be held forth in the first presentation remains strong.

18 **Aries Adjective** Themes Grouped
Compiled from a Base of about 751 words

Approaching (preliminary)
Expecting (approaching)
Preliminary (at the beginning)
Early (premature)

Beginning (starting)
Starting (beginning)
Founding (establishing)
Introductory (lead off)

Advancing (proceeding)
Moving Forward (advancing)
Proceeding (moving ahead)
Arriving (proceeding)

Addresses (greets)
Greets (welcomes)
Meets (greets)
Introduces (makes known)

Appoints (designates)
Identifies (labels)
Names (designates)
Designates (names)

Fresh (newly made)
New (pristine)
Mint (unused)

Unused (new)

Rushing (speeding)
Hurried (impatient)
Forcing (pushing)
Hasty (rushed)

Impulsive (rash)
Foolhardy (reckless)
Thoughtless (indiscreet)
Reckless (foolhardy)

Ardent (arousing)
Zealous (excited)
Eager (excited)
Arousing (inciting)

Positive (emphatic)
Certain (sure)
Presumptuous (arrogant)
Determined (positive)

Emphatic (insistent)
Insistent (emphatic)
Emphasized (featured)

Assertive (confronting)
Challenging (assertive)
Confronting (tackling)

Self-Centered (conceited)
Selfish (self-centered)
Self-Oriented (egotistical)

Dogmatic (opinionated)
Opinionated (close-minded)
Convinced (opinionated)

Curt (impolite)
Brusque (abrupt)
Impolite (discourteous)
Inconsiderate (thoughtless)

Empty (barren)
Naked (exposed)
Exposed (naked)
Vacant (empty)

Dry (arid)
Arid (dry)
Thirsty (dehydrated)

Dirty (begrimed)
Hairy (hirsute)
Smelly (ill-smelling)

66 Aries Adjective Theme Words Listed Alphabetically

Addresses (greets)
Advancing (proceeding)
Appoints (designates)
Approaching (preliminary)
Ardent (arousing)
Arid (dry)
Arousing (inciting)
Arriving (proceeding)
Assertive (confronting)
Beginning (starting)
Brusque (abrupt)
Certain (sure)
Challenging (assertive)
Confronting (tackling)

Convinced (opinionated)
Curt (impolite)
Designates (names)
Determined (positive)
Dirty (begrimed)
Dogmatic (opinionated)
Dry (arid)
Eager (excited)
Early (premature)
Emphasized (featured)
Emphatic (insistent)
Empty (barren)
Expecting (approaching)
Exposed (naked)

Foolhardy (reckless)
Forcing (pushing)
Founding (establishing)
Fresh (newly made)
Greets (welcomes)
Hairy (hirsute)
Hasty (rushed)
Hurried (impatient)
Identifies (labels)
Impolite (discourteous)
Impulsive (rash)
Inconsiderate (thoughtless)
Insistent (emphatic)
Introduces (makes known)
Introductory (lead off)
Meets (greets)
Mint (unused)
Moving Forward (advancing)
Naked (exposed)

Names (designates)
New (pristine)
Opinionated (close-minded)
Positive (emphatic)
Preliminary (at the beginning)
Presumptuous (arrogant)
Proceeding (moving ahead)
Reckless (foolhardy)
Rushing (speeding)
Self-Centered (conceited)
Self-Oriented (egotistical)
Selfish (self-centered)
Smelly (ill-smelling)
Starting (beginning)
Thirsty (dehydrated)
Thoughtless (indiscreet)
Unused (new)
Vacant (empty)
Zealous (excited)

Aries (Noun)

Aries (Noun) Essence

For Aries nouns beginnings start with anticipation, preview, or an indication. Aries nouns build urgency, perhaps a reckless haste, to define the start. There is a central foretaste or introduction before movement forward can proceed. Starts are not easy, and needed there is a show of boldness and courage to take on the challenges that are anticipated. If progress is slow then impatience along with rudeness may result. Empty places, especially those that are dry and arid, perhaps with dirt, are indicated.

The Aries noun emphasis remains on movement at the beginning, and a need for advancement off of the present status. Shows of impulsiveness, the need for immediacy of action, and a haste that can lead to unexpected out-comes, can occur. Aries nouns feed off the need to seek and respond to a challenge, even if they have to invent the circumstances that shape this. Behind the intentions of Aries nouns lies a motive for needing to move forward, to get off of the present indecision and lack of status.

Likely to show a self-centeredness and personal conceit that others do not take well toward, Aries nouns show a drive to continue to push ideas, plans and intentions forward. Aries nouns structure the world as revolving around self and their ideas. To effect their views pressure may be brought to bear. The Aries noun rashness to rush into decision is likely to be shown.

Urgency is a concept Aries nouns live by. Aries nouns show an impatience with those who cannot keep up with their movements and progress. The Aries nouns show a coerciveness, and apply pressure against others to meet their schedules. A show of personal power, with them at the center, is frequently a result and manifestation of the noun intentions.

Associations with and a mingling in empty places, with dry and arid conditions, and even a nakedness of self and surroundings is preferred. The odor of sweat, a hairy appearance, and a preference for dirty or muddy circumstances can be associated here.

13 **Aries Noun** Themes Grouped
Compiled from a Base of about 554 words

Indication (sign)
Foretaste (advance)
Anticipation (expectation)
Precursor (forerunner)

Approach (coming nearer)
Arrival (appearance)
Entrance (arrival)
Preview (advance showing)

Beginning (introduction)
Start (first step)
Introduction (familiarization)
Creation (beginning)

Movement (activity)
Advancement (motion forward))
Attempt (undertaking)
Action (movement)

Urgency (dire necessity)
Intensity (pushiness)
Emphasis (insistence)
Eagerness (urgency)

Impulsiveness (recklessness)
Haste (speed)
Recklessness (heedlessness)
Hurry (hastiness)

Boldness (daring)
Daring (fearlessness)
Courage (daring)
Audacity (forwardness)

Challenge (purpose)
Purpose (reason)
Motive (reason)
Reason (grounds)

Self-Centeredness (focus on self)
Conceit (egomania)
Egomania (excessive egotism)

Coercion (pressure)
Exclusion (show of power)
Imperative (command)
Imposition (pressuring)

Rashness (franticness)
Rudeness (impoliteness)
Impatience (rashness)
Impoliteness (rudeness)

Emptiness (barrenness)
Vacancy (emptiness or void)
Dryness (aridity)
Nakedness (barrenness)

Sweat (perspiration)
Smell (odor)

Filthiness (dirtiness)
Hairiness (hirsute)

51 **Aries Noun** Theme Words Listed Alphabetically

Action (movement)
Advancement (motion forward))
Anticipation (expectation)
Approach (coming nearer)
Arrival (appearance)
Attempt (undertaking)
Audacity (forwardness)
Beginning (introduction)
Boldness (daring)
Challenge (purpose)
Coercion (pressure)
Conceit (egomania)
Courage (daring)
Creation (beginning)
Daring (fearlessness)
Dryness (aridity)
Eagerness (urgency)
Egomania (excessive egotism)
Emphasis (insistence)
Emptiness (barrenness)
Entrance (arrival)
Exclusion (show of power)
Filthiness (dirtiness)
Foretaste (dirtiness)
Hairiness (hirsute)
Haste (speed)

Hurry (hastiness)
Impatience (rashness)
Imperative (command)
Impoliteness (rudeness)
Imposition (pressuring)
Impulsiveness (recklessness)
Indication (sign)
Intensity (pushiness)
Introduction (familiarization)
Motive (reason)
Movement (activity)
Nakedness (barrenness)
Precursor (forerunner)
Preview (advance showing)
Purpose (reason)
Rashness (franticness)
Reason (grounds)
Recklessness (heedlessness)
Rudeness (impoliteness)
Self-Centeredness (focus on self)
Smell (odor)
Start (first step)
Sweat (perspiration)
Urgency (dire necessity)
Vacancy (emptiness or void)

For Notations

Taurus

♉

Rulers: Yang Venus and Yin Psyche

Taurus (Adjective) **Essence**

Highlighted with Taurus adjectives is a practical and sensible attitude that arises out of a calm, relaxed and carefree approach. Taurus adjectives depict levels and depth to tolerance and patience. The Taurus adjective emphasis remains on productivity, growing and developing, especially with money and possessions. There can be a stubborn and hardheaded attitude toward responding to changes and opinions coming from others. But the idea of taking things slowly, being unhurried and relaxed reigns. This may also bring on an unimaginative outlook and keep them stuck in place.

To help life move forward smoothly matters need to be put forth in a practical and useful way. Adding complications to the flow of life is not the Taurus adjective way. Their emphasis is to remain conservative, conventional and focused on tangible results. They look for the development of productive and fruitful methods, which is why they can remain grounded, as in how things can be made to grow from the earth. This includes, of course, material benefits, like the growing and nurturing of financial assets, and keeping a sharp eye out for business opportunities that can turn a profit.

Taurus adjectives show a strong sense for being patient and long-suffering. They are able to bear up under pressures and distractions that would make others cringe, or perhaps run from any annoying interferences. Taurus adjectives bring on a carefree, untroubled front, and this goes to their core. Taurus adjectives show a dependability and steadiness for dealings with others, like when facing the pressures of daily life. Taurus adjectives show a need to keep life as uninvolved, moving along at a steady pace.

Taurus adjectives bring an innocence to living life, and are often surprised when others take their relaxed approach to matters in the wrong way. They present a spiritual objective to reasoning. Taurus adjectives show an attraction to inner objectives, and that an important part of life is about maintaining ties to nature and spirituality. Taurus adjectives show a deep yearning for understanding the non-physical side of existence.

23 **Taurus Adjective** Themes Grouped
Compiled from a Base of about 940 Words

Calm (collected)
Relaxed (laid-back)
Comfortable (relaxed)
Resting (relaxing)

Easygoing (calm)
Carefree (unconcerned)
Complacent (untroubled)
Serene (calm)

Still (unmoving)
Motionless (inactive)
Quiet (still)
Passive (tranquil)

Patient (long-suffering)
Enduring (long-lasting)
Tolerant (patient)

Dependable (reliable)
Stable (firm or steady)
Grounded (stable)
Reliable (dependable)

Practical (realistic)
Realistic (practical)
Expedient (fitting)
Sensible (rational)

Solid (dense)
Material (tangible)
Real (actual)
Touchable (tangible)

Simple (uninvolved)
Easy (effortless)
Effortless (uncomplicated)
Uncomplicated (simple)

Productive (fruitful)
Developing (growing)
Sustaining (prolonging)
Growing (maintaining)

Conservative (opposed to change)
Conventional (regular)
Orthodox (conventional)

Stubborn (obstinate)
Hardheaded (obstinate)
Inflexible (unyielding)
Obstinate (inflexible)

Inactive (still)
Slow (unhurried)
Lethargic (sluggish)
Lazy (slow-moving)

Unhurried (leisurely)
Leisurely (sluggish)
Lingering (unhurried)

Limp (unstiff)
Slack (drooping)
Loose (slack)

Money-Minded (seeks prosperity)
Materialistic (goods oriented)
Prosperous (flourishing)

Soon (impending)
Next (subsequent)
Following (next)
Forthcoming (impending)

Dull (unsharpened)
Blunt (dull, unsharp)
Unpointed (without a point)

Innocent (blameless)

Guileless (innocent)
Blameless (guiltless)

Awkward (clumsy)
Clumsy (lacking grace)
Ungainly (awkward)

Unimaginative (boring)
Dull-Witted (thickheaded)
Obtuse (dull witted)

Substantial (bulky or heavy)
Large (big in size, bulky)
Massive (gigantic)

Fleshy (fatty)
Chubby (plump)
Paunchy (fatty)

Small (little or tiny)
Slight (small)
Miniature (small)

82 **Taurus Adjective** Theme Words Listed Alphabetically

Awkward (clumsy)
Blameless (guiltless)
Blunt (dull)
Bulky (massive)
Calm (collected)
Carefree (unconcerned)
Chubby (plump)
Clumsy (lacking grace)
Comfortable (relaxed)
Complacent (untroubled)
Conservative (opposed to change)
Conventional (regular)
Dependable (reliable)
Developing (growing)
Dull (unsharpened)
Dull-Witted (thickheaded)
Easy (effortless)
Easygoing (calm)
Effortless (uncomplicated)
Enduring (long-lasting)
Expedient (fitting)
Fleshy (fatty)
Following (next)
Forthcoming (impending)
Grounded (stable)
Growing (maintaining)

Guileless (innocent)
Hardheaded (obstinate)
Inactive (still)
Inflexible (unyielding)
Innocent (blameless)
Large (big in size)
Lazy (slow-moving)
Leisurely (sluggish)
Lethargic (sluggish)
Limp (unstiff)
Lingering (unhurried)
Loose (slack)
Massive (gigantic)
Material (tangible)
Materialistic (goods oriented)
Miniature (small)
Money-Minded (prosperity seeking)
Motionless (inactive)
Next (subsequent)
Obstinate (inflexible)
Obtuse (dull witted)
Orthodox (conventional)
Passive (tranquil)
Patient (long-suffering)
Paunchy (fatty)
Practical (realistic)

Productive (fruitful)

Prosperous (flourishing)

Quiet (still)

Real (actual)

Realistic (practical)

Relaxed (laid-back)

Reliable (dependable)

Resting (relaxing)

Sensible (rational)

Serene (calm)

Simple (uninvolved)

Slack (drooping)

Slight (small)

Slow (unhurried)

Small (little or tiny)

Solid (firm)

Soon (impending)

Stable (firm or steady)

Still (unmoving)

Stubborn (obstinate)

Substantial (bulky or heavy)

Sustaining (prolonging)

Tolerant (patient)

Touchable (tangible)

Uncomplicated (simple)

Ungainly (awkward)

Unhurried (leisurely)

Unimaginative (boring)

Unpointed (pointless)

Unsharp (dull)

Taurus (Noun)

Taurus (Noun) Essence

Taurus nouns focus on moderation, consistency and great self-control. The need for regularity and conformity persists. Almost all action and activity is measured by monetary and material status. Sensations, touch, taste, feel, rule the decision-making processes. Often there is a size concern - either too big, or too small – and usually little in-between. Others with a different view can see their listlessness, bordering on being unskilled.

Taurus nouns focus on maintaining a steady and reliable path for progressing through life. The idea of having and retaining stability remains dominant, and moderation in all aspects is important. They indicate durability, want their possessions to be luxurious, but also to have a lasting quality. They generally are not into the latest fad, preferring instead to wait until the next fad reduces the prices of those previous "had to have" items.

Taurus nouns show a partiality toward uniformity and consistency within routine. They are not afraid of being a conformist. They can look at what is happening, and if this suits them then good, and if not they will move on to other scenarios. A clash of appearances or interests is not their way.

Leisure and luxury go together here. Taurus nouns show kindness, gentleness and tolerance, but tread on any of their core values and you can see the reaction from an angry bull. In momentary fits of rage they can bring tremendous amounts of destructive change. Taurus nouns do not emphasize outbursts. Moderation, uniformity and consistency remain central to the efforts described by Taurus nouns. Material substance and a lasting and enduring quality highlight the calm and steadiness desired.

Physical sensations can rule Taurus nouns. How does this taste? Does color add to this setting? What is that smell? How does that feel? Is it plush enough at my touch? What is that sound? Where is the musical and lyrical output that is needed? Feeling the earth go through their fingers, planting bushes and flowers for outside decoration, adding ornaments to enhance natural beauty – these are all matters that are shown by the Taurus nouns.

18 **Taurus Noun** Themes Grouped
Compiled from a Base of about 491 Words

Steadiness (composed)
Firmness (reliability)
Unchanging (unwavering)
Stability (firmness)

Practicality (usefulness)
Usefulness (serviceability)
Feasibility (workability)
Pragmatism (practicality)

Moderation (temperance)
Restraint (self-control)
Self-Control (restraint)
Temperance (moderation)

Uniformity (consistency)
Consistency (regularity)
Regularity (consistency)
Conformity (sameness)

Patience (tolerance)
Calmness (composure)
Tranquility (calm or quiet)
Serenity (tranquility)

Durability (toughness)
Endurance (holding out)
Toleration (forbearance)
Stamina (endurance)

Satisfaction (gratification)

Gratification (self-fulfillment)
Contentment (satisfaction)

Leisure Time (relaxation)
Intermission (breather)
Relaxation (taking it easy)

Earthy (natural)
Natural (unadulterated)
Organic (natural)

Sensations (perceptions)
Sensuality (carnality)
Feelings (touch sensations)

Finances (funds or capital)
Enrichment (becoming richer)
Thriving (flourishing)
Materialism (focus on values)

Stubbornness (willfulness)
Rigidity (firmness)
Inflexibility (rigidity)
Obstinacy (stubbornness)

Material (matter or stuff)
Substance (material or stuff)
Reality (actuality)
Matter (material)

Largeness (bigness)
Massive (bulky)

Fleshy (substantial)
Fatty (chubby)

Sturdiness (solidness)
Solidity (denseness)
Density (substance or solidity)
Bulk (mass or substance)

Listlessness (weariness)
Inactivity (motionless)

Immobility (fixity)

Ineptness (lacking skill)
Bungling (awkwardness)
Clumsiness (being ungraceful)

Stupidity (empty headedness)
Slowness (simple-mindedness)
Unskillful (inept)

65 **Taurus Noun** Theme Words Listed Alphabetically

Bulk (mass or substance)
Bungling (awkwardness)
Calmness (composure)
Clumsiness (being ungraceful)
Conformity (sameness)
Consistency (regularity)
Contentment (satisfaction)
Density (substance or solidity)
Durability (toughness)
Earthy (natural)
Endurance (holding out)
Enrichment (becoming richer)
Fatty (chubby)
Feasibility (workability)
Feelings (touch sensations)
Finances (funds or capital)

Firmness (reliability)
Fleshy (substantial)
Gratification (self-fulfillment)
Immobility (fixity)
Inactivity (motionless)
Ineptness (lacking skill)
Inflexibility (rigidity)
Intermission (breather)
Largeness (bigness)
Leisure Time (relaxation)
Listlessness (weariness)
Massive (bulky)
Material (matter or stuff)
Materialism (focus on values)
Matter (material)
Moderation (temperance)

Natural (unadulterated)
Obstinacy (stubbornness)
Organic (natural)
Patience (tolerance)
Practicality (usefulness)
Pragmatism (practicality)
Reality (actuality)
Regularity (consistency)
Relaxation (taking it easy)
Restraint (self-control)
Rigidity (firmness)
Satisfaction (gratification)
Self-Control (restraint)
Sensations (perceptions)
Sensuality (carnality)
Serenity (tranquility)
Slowness (simple-mindedness)

Solidity (denseness)
Stability (firmness)
Stamina (endurance)
Steadiness (composed)
Stubbornness (willfulness)
Stupidity (empty headedness)
Sturdiness (solidness)
Substance (material or stuff)
Temperance (moderation)
Thriving (flourishing)
Toleration (forbearance)
Tranquility (calm or quiet)
Unchanging (unwavering)
Uniformity (consistency)
Unskillful (inept)
Usefulness (serviceability)

For Notations

Gemini

Rulers: Yang Mercury and Yin Vulcan

Gemini (Adjective) **Essence**

Communication and being able to express ideas in understandable and varied ways is emphasized through the Gemini adjectives. Gemini adjectives can be verbose, so expect many words. There is herein an underlying curiosity that works to increase intelligence and knowledge. This development is normally spurred by self-learning, study and/or schooling. Determining what is knowable reigns, and becoming familiar with available resources so that self and others can observe facts is a steady pursuit. There is a duality, a pairing, and often things appear in twos. There is also an emphasis on what is handy or nearby. Being adaptable and flexible highlights the need here to have interactive communication open at all times.

Gemini adjectives highlight the asking of questions, and come with an innate curiosity that seeks to understand all sides of a matter. Often the answers to questions raised and discussed just lead to more questions and the seeking of additional clarification or answers. Shown is an interest in schooling, and the learning processes. Study remains important, and as new facts or insight are discovered, this can lead to more questions, each needing additional research and answers. The face of an academic lingers here.

Determining the basis of facts, where they come from, how they originated, whether they lead to logical conclusions or do more to muddle understanding, is a continual pursuit. It becomes necessary to be conversant with the many variations of a subject. The pursuit of knowledge and learning highlight a continual interest in many subject matters. Included is the ability to notice, even be intrigued by, details others fail to see.

Gemini adjectives show an importance to remain up to date with the facts, keeping up with what is going on, or with neighbors. The idea of remaining conversant with the current flow of information, gossip even, remains important. There is a preference to be informed about changes, what is happening, and how matters are unfolding and coming across to others as well. Gemini adjectives bring out an innate curiosity.

16 **Gemini Adjective** Themes Grouped
Compiled from a Base of about 615 Words

Talkative (gabby)
Articulate (talkative)
Eloquent (articulate)
Vocal (spoken)

Explains (clarifies)
Describes (explains)
Illustrates (pictures)
Narrates (explains)

Curious (inquisitive)
Inquisitive (curious)
Asking (inquisitive)
Questioning (asking)

Intelligent (brilliant)
Smart (intelligent)
Bright (literate)
Schooled (instructed)

Familiar with (conversant)
Informed about (knows about)
Wise to (informed about)

Thinking (deliberating)
Reasoning (thinking through)
Contemplative (cerebral)

Academic (schooled)
Literate (well-versed)
Educational (instructional)
Scholarly (academic)

Learnable (knowable)
Verifiable (determinable)
Determinable (verifiable)
Knowable (learnable)

Discussing (mentioning)
Revealing (disclosing)
Mentioning (discussing)

Sees (observes)
Notices (sees)
Records (documents)
Observes (notices)

Explicit (distinct)
Understandable (lucid)
Distinct (explicit)
Legible (clear)

Similar (alike)
Alike (similar)
Duplicated (repeated)
Related (similar)

Imitative (mimicking)
Mimicking (copying)
Gesturing (motioning)
Motioning (signaling)

Handy (accessible)
Adjacent (adjoining)
Local (near)
Nearby (close by)

Double (accommodates two)
Twin (doubled)
Redundant (repetitive)
Paired (coupled)

Flexible (bendable)
Pliable (flexible)
Bendable (adjustable)

60 **Gemini Adjective** Theme Words Listed Alphabetically

Academic (schooled)
Adjacent (adjoining)
Alike (similar)
Articulate (talkative)
Asking (inquisitive)
Bendable (adjustable)
Bright (literate)
Contemplative (cerebral)
Curious (inquisitive)
Describes (explains)
Determinable (verifiable)
Discussing (mentioning)
Distinct (explicit)
Double (accommodates two)
Duplicated (repeated)
Educational (instructional)
Eloquent (articulate)
Explains (clarifies)

Explicit (distinct)
Familiar with (conversant)
Flexible (bendable)
Gesturing (motioning)
Handy (accessible)
Illustrates (pictures)
Imitative (mimicking)
Informed about (knows about)
Inquisitive (curious)
Intelligent (brilliant)
Knowable (learnable)
Learnable (knowable)
Legible (clear)
Literate (well-versed)
Local (near)
Mentioning (discussing)
Mimicking (copying)
Motioning (signaling)

Narrates (explains)
Nearby (close by)
Notices (sees)
Observes (notices)
Paired (coupled)
Pliable (flexible)
Questioning (asking)
Reasoning (thinking through)
Records (documents)
Redundant (repetitive)
Related (similar)
Revealing (disclosing)
Scholarly (academic)

Schooled (instructed)
Sees (observes)
Similar (alike)
Smart (intelligent)
Talkative (gabby)
Thinking (deliberating)
Twin (doubled)
Understandable (lucid)
Verifiable (determinable)
Vocal (spoken)
Wise to (informed about)

Gemini (Noun)

Gemini (Noun) Essence

Gemini nouns are focused on the interchange of information, and gesturing while talking is an important means of doing this. Somehow, internally, the gestures add a punctuation to the meaning of their verbal output. Gemini nouns are driven to convey the importance of their ideas and messages to others. Sending signals using both words and gestures becomes a trademark here. But there is more to talk than just conversation. There also has to be back and forth exchanges that can continue for long periods until those involved are satisfied.

Communication and clarification, getting facts straight, interpreting them accurately, etc., is stressed within the Gemini nouns. Noting the resemblance amongst objects or people, applying ingenuity and cleverness to daily actions, using their inherent flexibility and ability to adapt to and also to observe life become a point of emphasis. These can lead to ongoing schooling or self-learning. The creation of replicas and images that are similar is often stressed and the idea of duality persists.

Clarity of getting their ideas across, and developing fluency with language, occupies much of the Gemini nouns emphasis. Gemini nouns show a pride with their ability to master difficult intellectual tasks. In a work place they may become the "reference" person others seek for answers. Often their talking can deteriorate to gibbering, trash talk, and just ongoing wordiness. Few others can out-talk the Gemini noun emphasis. Gemini nouns have the words, and they want you to know that they have them. But their focus does not just remain on words. It remains on using communication effectively to get their ideas, intentions and messages across.

For Gemini nouns learning is a process that never stops. They portray an innate cleverness along with a crafty way of turning ideas and situations around to make them noticeable and unique. They can be mercurial, flexible, and shifty. Gemini nouns display a nimbleness of both mind and body, enabling changes in direction with thoughts as well as movement. Yet, overriding here is their emphasis on curiosity. Curiosity, reasoning, communication, conversation, eloquence and observation dominate here.

12 **Gemini Noun** Themes Grouped
Compiled from a Base of about 557 Words

Communication (exchange of information)
Information (message)
Signal (communication)
Announcement (communication)

Conversation (talk)
Discussion (talking)
Dialog (conversation)
Talk (discussion)

Clarification (explanation)
Explanation (account)
Interpretation (clarification)
Description (portrayal)

Eloquence (fluency)
Fluency (command of language)
Talking (jabberer)
Glibness (wordiness)

Similarity (resemblance)
Resemblance (similarity)
Duplication (reproduction)
Redundancy (duplication)

Cleverness (ingenuity)
Craftiness (know-how)
Proficiency (know-how)
Skillfulness (handiness)

Agility (nimbleness)
Flexibility (suppleness)
Nimbleness (agility)
Adaptability (flexibility)

Reasoning (working things out)
Cogitation (thinking)
Thinking (brainwork)
Logic (reasoning)

Curiosity (questioning)
Inquisitiveness (curiosity)
Observance (noticing)
Questioning (curiosity)

Education (schooling)
Learning (studying)
Study (learning)
Schooling (learning)

Convenience (handiness)
Handiness (convenience)
Nearness (proximity)

Duality (replica)
Reflection (mirroring)
Replica (likeness)

46 **Gemini Noun** Theme Words Listed Alphabetically

Adaptability (flexibility)
Agility (nimbleness)
Announcement (communication)
Clarification (explanation)
Cleverness (ingenuity)
Cogitation (thinking)
Communication (exchange of information)
Convenience (handiness)
Conversation (talk)
Craftiness (know-how)
Curiosity (questioning)
Description (portrayal)
Dialog (conversation)
Discussion (talking)
Duality (replica)
Duplication (reproduction)
Education (schooling)
Eloquence (fluency)
Explanation (account)
Flexibility (suppleness)
Fluency (command of language)
Glibness (wordiness)
Handiness (convenience)
Information (message)

Inquisitiveness (curiosity)
Interpretation (clarification)
Learning (studying)
Logic (reasoning)
Nearness (proximity)
Nimbleness (agility)
Observance (noticing)
Proficiency (know-how)
Questioning (curiosity)
Reasoning (working things out)
Redundancy (duplication)
Reflection (mirroring)
Replica (likeness)
Resemblance (similarity)
Schooling (learning)
Signal (communication)
Similarity (resemblance)
Skillfulness (handiness)
Study (learning)
Talk (discussion)
Talking (jabberer)
Thinking (brainwork)

For Notations

Cancer

♋

Rulers: Yang Moon and Yin Sun

Cancer (Adjective) Essence

The Cancer adjective themes focus on the importance of sentiment and emotion. Playing out the scenarios of life as melodramatic exercises, exhibiting the raw emotion behind their intentions, and yet at the same time trying to hide innate insecurities and vulnerabilities. Often this is done by over-achieving in certain areas of life, the idea being that if one can achieve a high level of progress then others should recognize their merits.

Cancer adjectives show a strong emphasis within on preservation, care, maintaining the status quo, and holding and nurturing. Concepts concerning home, family, country and what these represent are highlighted. Local regions, land, surrounding areas, and the impact or potential of these remain recognized. Standout and cherished memories from early life usually play an important part in the unfolding of life's potential. Hoarding, acquiring. nurturing and the keeping of possessions, too, are most likely to have their role. Cancer adjectives hold history and its impact on life as important. Digestion and the stomach are emphasized.

Cancer adjectives show a need for keeping one's guard up and ensuring that self, family, and those cherished are protected in all ways. This can often dominate the Cancer adjective role. Cancer adjectives are into preserving the status quo, and are likely to very strongly resist suggestions that "new" ways are better than "old" ways. The keeping of mementoes, memories, and items that bring back those former ideas of the closeness remembered and cherished remain important. Cancer adjectives show a need for an indirect or sideways approach to meeting life and people.

Parenting, protecting, watching over the children, and preserving the family memories are important. The water, oceans, moisture, and porous items that hold water also remain in focus. What was customary in the past needs to remain defined and honored even today – an important focus within the Cancer adjective words.

26 **Cancer Adjective** Themes Grouped
Compiled from a Base of about 839 Words

Emotional (sentimental)
Sentimental (emotional)
Melodramatic (emotional)
Nostalgic (sentimental)

Vulnerable (insecure)
Exposed (vulnerable)
Undefended (defenseless)
Unprotected (unguarded)

Nearest (closest)
Close (nearest)
Internal (inward)
Inward (interior)

Guarded (protected)
Protective (shielding)
Defensive (protective)
Shielding (protective)

Preserving (conserving)
Keeping (saving)
Maintaining (keeping)
Remembering (not forgetting)

Moody (fickle)
Disagreeable (irritable)
Cranky (moody)
Grouchy (irritable)

Household (domestic)
Patriotic (nationalistic)
Residential (domestic)
Domestic (home loving)

Parental (maternal or paternal)
Holding (embracing)
Nurturing (mothering)
Touching (caressing)

Dependent on (relying on)
Subject to (dependent on)
Conditional (hinging on)

Cherished (esteemed)
Memorable (notable)
Noteworthy (memorable)
Beloved (cherished)

Historical (ancient)
Classical (traditional)
Traditional (customary)
Bygone (past)

Native (indigenous)
Provincial (regional)
Local (provincial)
Regional (provincial)

Rustic (rural)
Rural (country)
Countrified (rural)
Downhome (countrified)

Exterior (outside)
Outside (exterior)
Peripheral (outside)

Edible (eatable)
Consumable (ingestible)

Digestible (edible)
Ingesting (eating)

Sidewise (indirect)
Indirect (sidewise)

Amasses (collects)
Hoards (collects)
Collects (accumulates)
Purchases (obtains)

Grasping (gripping)
Possessive (acquisitive)
Clings to (holds)
Clutches (grasps)

Secures (attaches)
Closes (secures)
Fastens (secures)
Attaches (secures)

Woven (interlaced)
Latticed (grilled)
Fibrous (stringy or wiry)
Netlike (meshed)

Furry (fuzzy)

Woolly (fleecy)
Shaggy (fuzzy)

Marshy (watery)
Absorbs (soaks in)
Soggy (waterlogged)
Drenched (saturated)

Adhesive (clinging)
Sticky (gummy or tacky)
Slimy (viscous)
Gummy (sticky)

Scaly (flaky)
Crumbly (flaky)
Powdery (granulated)
Flaking (peeling)

Notched (toothed)
Toothed (serrated)
Pitted (pock marked)
Zigzagged (serrated)

Leakproof (impervious)
Watertight (impermeable)
Impervious (leakproof)

98 **Cancer Adjective** Theme Words Listed Alphabetically

Absorbs (soaks in)
Adhesive (glue)
Amasses (collects)
Attaches (secures)
Beloved (cherished)
Bygone (past)
Cherished (esteemed)
Classical (traditional)
Clings to (holds)
Close (nearest)
Closes (secures)
Clutches (grasps)
Collects (accumulates)
Conditional (hinging on)
Consumable (ingestible)
Countrified (rural)
Cranky (moody)
Crumbly (flaky)
Defensive (protective)
Dependent on (relying on)
Digestible (edible)
Disagreeable (irritable)
Domestic (home loving)
Downhome (countrified)
Drenched (saturated)
Edible (eatable)
Emotional (sentimental)
Exposed (vulnerable)
Exterior (outside)

Fastens (secures)
Fibrous (stringy or wiry)
Flaking (peeling)
Furry (fuzzy)
Grasping (gripping)
Grouchy (irritable)
Guarded (protected)
Gummy (sticky)
Historical (ancient)
Hoards (collects)
Holding (embracing)
Household (domestic)
Impervious (leakproof)
Indirect (sidewise)
Ingesting (eating)
Internal (inward)
Inward (interior)
Keeping (saving)
Latticed (grilled)
Leakproof (impervious)
Local (provincial)
Maintaining (keeping)
Marshy (watery)
Melodramatic (emotional)
Memorable (notable)
Moody (fickle)
Native (indigenous)
Nearest (closest)
Netlike (meshed)

Nostalgic (sentimental)
Notched (toothed)
Noteworthy (memorable)
Nurturing (mothering)
Outside (exterior)
Parental (maternal or paternal)
Patriotic (nationalistic)
Peripheral (outside)
Pitted (pock marked)
Possessive (acquisitive)
Powdery (granulated)
Preserving (conserving)
Protective (shielding)
Provincial (regional)
Purchases (obtains)
Regional (provincial)
Remembering (not forgetting)
Residential (domestic)
Rural (country)
Rustic (rural)

Scaly (flaky)
Secures (attaches)
Sentimental (emotional)
Shaggy (fuzzy)
Shielding (protective)
Sidewise (indirect)
Slimy (viscous)
Soggy (waterlogged)
Sticky (gummy or tacky)
Subject to (dependent on)
Toothed (serrated)
Touching (caressing)
Traditional (customary)
Undefended (defenseless)
Unprotected (unguarded)
Vulnerable (insecure)
Watertight (impermeable)
Woolly (fleecy)
Woven (interlaced)
Zigzagged (serrated)

Cancer (Noun)

Cancer (Noun) Essence

Cancer nouns show a focus on protection, offering safe conduct, and safeguarding those persons or possessions that are in their care. There is a need for preservation and keeping an alert watch to insure that people and possessions remain safe and cherished in appropriate ways. Physical and even emotional barriers, perhaps inner, may be constructed to ensure protection. Hiding behind or using emotional protective barriers though may indicate inner psychological problems or needs.

Ensuring that there are adequate resources available, that the home is safe and protected, and that possession and occupancy are assured, is emphasized. Cancer nouns prefer to remain vigilant, watchful, and aware of their surroundings. Changes as they occur there may be taken as warning signs. The neighborhood, family memories, nostalgia, ancestry, and established customs are remembered. Nourishment and subsistence for self and family are emphasized. Cancer nouns can indicate that there can be a hard exterior shell covering what could be much vulnerability.

Housing, shelter, and occupancy are areas that are related to the needs for offering protection, and are seriously highlighted within the Cancer noun themes. Accumulating necessary items, things to be held aside in case of future or potential needs, are also found within this word base. Consumption and the use of goods remain important. So too ideas involving cooking and the preparing of nourishing food are highlighted. Offering subsistence to keep others well and healthy remains important.

Shelters and housing, accommodations, are needed for their interest in the accumulation of possessions. This can affect the spaces needed for general occupancy and living matters, but somehow such can all be worked out to an amiable end. Often there may be a focus on having a hobby, adding to items in that hobby, and taking pride in the thoroughness of what has been accumulated and how their items have been preserved.

Significant here is the need for emotional responses and outlets. There is a need to express emotions in ways that have a meaningful impact.

27 **Cancer Noun** Themes Grouped
Compiled from a Base of about 949 Words

Protection (safe conduct)
Defense (protection)
Safeguarding (protecting)
Preservation (saving)

Watchfulness (alertness)
Alertness (watchfulness)
Precaution (safeguard)
Safety (keeping watchfulness)

Dependence (reliance on)
Reliance (dependence)
Attachment (reliance)

Barricade (deterrent)
Stronghold (fortification)
Fortification (stronghold)

Sticking (holding)
Securing (fastening)
Closing (securing)
Fastening (closing)
Grasping (holding on)

Parenting (raising offspring)
Nurturing (giving protection)
Safekeeping (having responsibility)
Cherishing (holding dear)

Shelter (housing)
Housing (lodgings)
Home (residence)
Accommodation (shelter)

Occupancy (tenancy)
Possession (holding or tenure)
Ownership (possession)
Tenancy (occupation)

Consumption (use of goods)
Absorption (consummation)
Depletion (using up)

Accumulation (bringing in)
Bringing In (collecting)
Saving (collecting)
Hoarding (stockpiling)

Emotional Responses (outlets)
Sentiment (feelings or attitude)
Melodrama (sentimental drama)
Affection (feeling)

Moodiness (emotional feelings)
Irritability (testiness)
Crabbiness (grouchiness)
Brooding (moping)

Component (source)
Contents (components)
Piece (component or morsel)
Source (basis)
Insides (inner parts)

Cooking (preparing food)
Nourishment (sustenance)
Subsistence (provisions)
Digestive Processes

Family (family members)
Parentage (ancestry)
Ancestry (lineage)
Descendants (offspring)

Memories (reminders)
Emotional Closeness (attachment)
Reminders (mementos)
Mementos (keepsakes)

Nostalgia (remembering)
Custom (convention)
Patriotism (nationalism)
Memorial (monument)
Flag (national emblem)
Land (one's nation)

Neighborhood (area)
Environs (surroundings)
Land (your property)
Territory (area or region)

Agriculture (farming)
Farming (growing)
Rural Practices (agriculture)
Crop Raising (farming)

Notch (mark)
Pit (dent or groove)
Cavity (pit or hole)
Indentation (depression)

Fuzz (nap or thatch)
Fur (hairy covering)
Wool (fleece or fuzz)
Thatch (hair)
Beard (whiskers)

Exterior (covering)
Covering (exterior)
Outer Shell (covering)
Facade (exterior part)

Weaving (interlacing)
Lattice (woven work)
Overlay (overlap)

Sogginess (wetness)
Saturation (wetness)
Irrigation (wetting)
Wetness (sogginess)

Sidewise Motion (indirectness)

Watertight (leakproof)

Leakproof (watertight)

Sealed (watertight)

Scales (laminar coating)

Fragments (fine grains or dust)

Dust (fine-grained material)

Powder (dust or fine grains)

105 **Cancer Noun** Theme Words Listed Alphabetically

Absorption (consummation)
Accommodation (shelter)
Accumulation (bringing in)
Affection (feeling)
Agriculture (farming)
Alertness (watchfulness)
Ancestry (lineage)
Attachment (reliance)
Barricade (deterrent)
Beard (whiskers)
Bringing In (collecting)
Brooding (moping)
Cavity (pit or hole)
Cherishing (holding dear)
Closing (securing)
Component (source)
Consumption (use of goods)
Contents (components)
Cooking (preparing food)
Covering (exterior)
Crabbiness (grouchiness)
Crop Raising (farming)
Custom (convention)

Defense (protection)
Dependence (reliance on)
Depletion (using up)
Descendants (offspring)
Digestive Processes
Dust (fine-grained material)
Emotional Closeness (attachment)
Emotional Responses (outlets)
Environs (surroundings)
Exterior (covering)
Facade (exterior part)
Family (family members)
Farming (growing)
Fastening (closing)
Flag (national emblem)
Fortification (stronghold)
Fragments (fine grains or dust)
Fur (hairy covering)
Fuzz (nap or thatch)
Grasping (holding on)
Hoarding (stockpiling)
Home (residence)
Housing (lodgings)

Indentation (depression)
Insides (inner parts)
Irrigation (wetting)
Irritability (testiness)
Land (one's nation)
Land (your property)
Lattice (woven work)
Leakproof (watertight)
Melodrama (sentimental drama)
Mementos (keepsakes)
Memorial (monument)
Memories (reminders)
Moodiness (emotional feelings)
Neighborhood (area)
Nostalgia (remembering)
Notch (mark)
Nourishment (sustenance)
Nurturing (giving protection)
Occupancy (tenancy)
Outer Shell (covering)
Overlay (overlap)
Ownership (possession)
Parentage (ancestry)
Parenting (raising offspring)
Patriotism (nationalism)
Piece (component or morsel)
Pit (dent or groove)
Possession (holding or tenure)
Powder (dust or fine grains)
Precaution (safeguard)

Preservation (saving)
Protection (safe conduct)
Reliance (dependence)
Reminders (mementos)
Rural Practices (agriculture)
Safeguarding (protecting)
Safekeeping (having responsibility)
Safety (keeping watchfulness)
Saturation (wetness)
Saving (collecting)
Scales (laminar coating)
Sealed (watertight)
Securing (fastening)
Sentiment (feelings or attitude)
Shelter (housing)
Sidewise Motion (indirectness)
Sogginess (wetness)
Source (basis)
Sticking (holding)
Stronghold (fortification)
Subsistence (provisions)
Tenancy (occupation)
Territory (area or region)
Thatch (hair)
Watchfulness (alertness)
Watertight (leakproof)
Weaving (interlacing)
Wetness (sogginess)
Wool (fleece or fuzz)

Leo

Rulers: Yang Sun and Yin Moon

Leo (Adjective) Essence

Leo adjectives show the dignified ways that attitudes and feelings can be put across. Leo adjectives highlight the showing off of a noble and aristocratic presence that can make those with these words strong stand out amongst others. Leo adjectives come along with a spontaneity and natural-ness that can leave a positive lasting impression on those around them. Leo adjectives also allow an instinctive warmth and cheerfulness.

Leo adjectives show an urge for drama and expression that plays out with affection and good-natured camaraderie. Included here is a noble and dignified demeanor, along with a cheerful and frolicsome front, all put on spontaneously of course, that can bring on popularity. But behind this lies a pretension about ideas of reality, augmented by boasts of prowess and conspicuous flaunts. Flattery comes easily, along sometimes with a stuck-up and pompous attitude.

A sense of being affectionate and loving shows strong in the Leo adjectives. Along with this show of affection comes an inner warmth that spreads among others easily. Within the Leo adjective energies lies a need for display, the drive to be conspicuous, even flamboyant, in some way. Leo adjectives show a good nature that shines through despite sometimes having doubts about self and life's role. It is this show of warmth and affection that highlights the Leo adjectives. Leo adjectives include way of acting, usually in a spontaneous manner, that brings an ability to hold the attention of those around through unforced reactions.

This can come at a price though. Being dashy and showy, showing affection and warmth, can also be mixed in with assumed posturing and attitudes. Such can come across as imperious and lordly, boastful and proud, even arrogant. Sometimes vanity can be overpowering and not have the suave influence expected from the Leo adjectives. Leo adjectives show a need to be audacious and conspicuous, along with easy spontaneity.

16 Leo Adjective Themes Grouped
Compiled from a Base of about 671 Words

Dramatic (theatrical)
Entertaining (amusing)
Expressive (spontaneous)
Amusing (entertaining)

Affectionate (loving)
Good-Natured (amiable)
Warm (hospitable)
Loving (affectionate)

Notable (remarkable)
Glorified (praised)
Proud (self-contented)
Famous (eminent)

Dignified (distinguished)
Imposing (dignified)
Noble (distinguished)
Aristocratic (dignified)

Cheerful (gleeful)
Playful (frolicsome)
Frolicsome (playful)

Spontaneous (extemporaneous)
Natural (spontaneous)
Unforced (natural)

Dashing (showy)
Stylish (classy or high-toned)

Chic (fashionable)
Dapper (neat)

Feigned (pretended)
Pretended (assumed)
Claimed (alleged)
Assumed (pretended)

Imperious (lordly)
Lordly (boastful)
Boastful (bragging)
Vain (proud)

Pompous (high-sounding)
Egotistical (self-important)
Smug (complacent)
Arrogant (smug)

Insincere (phony)
Patronizing (condescending)
Phony (insincere)

Flaunted (displayed)
Conspicuous (prominent)
Flagrant (audacious)
Blatant (conspicuous)

Ornate (elaborate)
Flowery (ornate)
Garish (gaudy)

Flamboyant (showy)

Foppish (pompous)
Dandyish (showy)
Stuck-up (pompous)

Flattering (laudatory)
Praising (flattering)

Fawning (flattering)

Swollen (distended)
Lumpy (uneven)
Protruding (showing)
Crested (ridged)

59 **Leo Adjective** Theme Words Listed Alphabetically

Affectionate (loving)
Amusing (entertaining)
Aristocratic (dignified)
Arrogant (smug)
Assumed (pretended)
Blatant (conspicuous)
Boastful (bragging)
Cheerful (gleeful)
Chic (fashionable)
Claimed (alleged)
Conspicuous (prominent)
Crested (ridged)
Dandyish (showy)
Dapper (neat)
Dashing (showy)
Dignified (distinguished)
Dramatic (theatrical)
Egotistical (self-important)
Entertaining (amusing)
Expressive (spontaneous)

Famous (eminent)
Fawning (flattering)
Feigned (pretended)
Flagrant (audacious)
Flamboyant (showy)
Flattering (laudatory)
Flaunted (displayed)
Flowery (ornate)
Foppish (pompous)
Frolicsome (playful)
Garish (gaudy)
Glorified (praised)
Good-Natured (amiable)
Imperious (lordly)
Imposing (dignified)
Insincere (phony)
Lordly (boastful)
Loving (affectionate)
Lumpy (uneven)
Natural (spontaneous)

Noble (distinguished)
Notable (remarkable)
Ornate (elaborate)
Patronizing (condescending)
Phony (insincere)
Playful (frolicsome)
Pompous (high-sounding)
Praising (flattering)
Pretended (assumed)
Protruding (showing)

Proud (self-contented)
Smug (complacent)
Spontaneous (extemporaneous)
Stuck-up (pompous)
Stylish (classy or high-toned)
Swollen (distended)
Unforced (natural)
Vain (proud)
Warm (hospitable)

Leo (Noun)

♌

Leo (Noun) Essence

The Leo noun emphasis depicts an ability to bring passion, fervor and excitement into play. This brings an intensity of spirit, a vitality that can be called upon to help augment and emphasize the passions of the moment. Getting into the close association of passion and affection is a Leo noun trait. The ability to add a liveliness, verve, and intensity of emotion lies within the Leo nouns. If you want to add excitement, and to bring passion to the moment, then draw upon the energies within the Leo nouns for this.

Leo nouns bring passion and warmth that enhance showing dramatic expression, along with all of the theatrics and emotion this entails. There usually is a naturalness to this expression, and accepting praise and taking in adulation is welcomed. There can be an arrogance, and a pride that borders on insincerity. A display of clothing, style and sophistication also follows. Some shows of cowardice and timidity can appear.

Achieving prominence while maintaining a stately and dignified manner shows strong in the Leo noun attributes. Leo nouns show a strong driving need to strive for and achieve popularity, to remain conspicuous within one's area of experience. A play to the audience may be made, with the intention that the appreciation and recognition that comes back enhances one's reputation. There very well may be a pursuit for renown.

But the Leo noun essence is able to bring more than passion and intensity into focus, there can be a naturalness and spontaneity to add festivity, hospitality and abandon to any occasion. There is an emphasis on entertainment, of getting others, an audience, involved in the unfolding of a story, a drama, or a tale of life. Here you can find passions running wild with excitement, and an enthusiasm that is infectious and brings out the best in others, while also adding to the enjoyment of the moment. Just don't let laziness or lethargy take hold.

Within the Leo noun keywords comes an emphasis on style to highlight appearance that draws upon the latest apparel or colors in vogue. For Leo nouns it remains important to be associated with the current trends.

14 **Leo Noun** Themes Grouped
Compiled from a Base of about 722 Words

Affection (emotion)
Ardor (affection)
Passion (emotion)
Intimacy (close association)
Warmth (affection)

Drama (showmanship)
Expression (emotion)
Emotion (expression)
Theatrics (showmanship)

Embellishment (pretense)
Coloration (fabrication)
Fabrication (embellishment)
Boasting (bragging)

Naturalness (spontaneity)
Festivity (celebration)
Cheer (high spirits)
Spontaneity (naturalness)

Praise (acclaim)
Adulation (praise)
Acclaim (approval)
Glorification (honoring)
Exaltation (praise)

Entertainment (amusement)
Recreation (entertainment)
Diversion (recreation)

Frolic (gaiety)

Arrogance (pride)
Pride (self-importance)
Conceit (pride)
Vanity (egotism)

Insincerity (phoniness)
Pretense (pretending)
Flattery (false compliment)
Phoniness (insincerity)

Dignity (stateliness)
Prominence (conspicuousness)
Popularity (recognition)
Distinction (renown)

Display (exhibition)
Lavishness (extravagance)
Ostentation (display)
Gaudiness (garishness)

Nattiness (style)
Stylishness (popular mannerism)
Sophistication (worldliness)

Laziness (idleness)
Idleness (lethargy)
Drowsiness (sleepiness)

Cowardice (timidity)
Timidity (cowardice)

Childbirth (beginnings)
Offspring (issue)

Swelling (bulge)
Bulge (lump)
Protrusion (projection)

55 Leo Noun Theme Words Listed Alphabetically

Acclaim (approval)
Adulation (praise)
Affection (emotion)
Ardor (affection)
Arrogance (pride)
Boasting (bragging)
Bulge (lump)
Cheer (high spirits)
Childbirth (beginnings)
Coloration (fabrication)
Conceit (pride)
Cowardice (timidity)
Dignity (stateliness)
Display (exhibition)
Distinction (renown)
Diversion (recreation)
Drama (showmanship)
Drowsiness (sleepiness)
Embellishment (pretense)
Emotion (expression)
Entertainment (amusement)

Exaltation (praise)
Expression (emotion)
Fabrication (embellishment)
Festivity (celebration)
Flattery (false compliment)
Frolic (gaiety)
Gaudiness (garishness)
Glorification (honoring)
Idleness (lethargy)
Insincerity (phoniness)
Intimacy (close association)
Lavishness (extravagance)
Laziness (idleness)
Nattiness (style)
Naturalness (spontaneity)
Offspring (issue)
Ostentation (display)
Passion (emotion)
Phoniness (insincerity)
Popularity (recognition)
Praise (acclaim)
Pretense (pretending)

Pride (self-importance)
Prominence (conspicuousness)
Protrusion (projection)
Recreation (entertainment)
Sophistication (worldliness)
Spontaneity (naturalness)
Stylishness (popular mannerism)

Swelling (bulge)
Theatrics (showmanship)
Timidity (cowardice)
Vanity (egotism)
Warmth (affection)

Virgo

♍

Rulers: Yang Vulcan and Yin Mercury

Virgo (Adjective) Essence

Virgo adjectives center on offering support, being helpful, providing supplies as needed, and maintaining exacting standards. There is an emphasis on giving aid and assistance, helping out, and standing by ready to offer support. Allied with this is an attention to duty - that is the strong thrust to directly attend to matters that have been assumed as obligations. There is a need to remain aware of what duties have remained as a focus, and also how to attend to those duties in a manner that is befitting. This implies retaining a faithful devotion to such obligations.

Attention to detail, remaining loyal and dutiful, an orderly and neat approach to arrangement, and a need to classify and organize information and data are noted in the Virgo adjectives. Remaining factual and clear with details, ensuring that there are distinct delineations among topics, and looking for genuine and unblemished items feature strongly. Ceremony and ritual remain important. Critical remarks and a fussy adherence to standards are also shown here.

Neatness and tidiness remain important. Order has to be maintained down to each individual part. Without a meticulous and selective attention to detail, acquiring neatness to the level desired is difficult to achieve. Tidying up, keeping matters and objects in their necessary order, even making changes to that order when that becomes necessary, are highlighted. The need to be and remain proper extends to being virtuous, i.e., following a standard of modesty, perhaps embodying that in a religious theme or ritual.

For Virgo adjectives discrimination about, fussiness with detail, and the need to keep matters and information in their place is strong. All neatly categorized and available in a logical way, even to an exacting personal standard to satisfy current demands. Preparing itemized lists, rearranging the orders to ensure a logical unfolding, and then following that arrangement though to help ease the path through life are also a part of Virgo adjectives.

22 **Virgo Adjective** Themes Grouped
Compiled from a Base of about 727 Words

Constructive (helpful)
Helpful (aiding)
Supportive (helpful)
Aiding (assisting)

Dutiful (conscientious)
Faithful (dutiful)
Attentive (faithful)
Devoted (attentive)

Meticulous (exacting)
Selective (fastidious)
Fastidious (exacting)
Exacting (painstaking)

Neat (tidy)
Orderly (arranged)
Aligned (neat)
Tidy (neat or orderly)

Classifies (organizes)
Organizes (classifies)
Discriminates (distinguishes)
Itemizes (lists)

Factual (faithful to)
Accurate (factual)
Exact (factual)
Precise (explicit)

Explicit (clear)
Clear (explicit)
Unambiguous (explicit)
Distinct (clear)

Holy (pious)
Saintly (pious)
Religious (holy)
Blessed (sainted)

Virtuous (chaste)
Chaste (virginal)
Innocent (virtuous)
Modest (proper)

Certified (authentic)
Genuine (legal or real)
Unmarked (undefaced)
Correct (genuine)

Supplies (equips)
Equips (furnishes)
Furnishes (provides)
Stocks (furnishes)

Component (part of)
Segment (portion)
Part of (component)
Fractional (partial)

Ceremonial (formal)
Formal (proper)
Proper (formal)
Solemn (ceremonial)

Trains (practices)
Practices (trains)
Uses (trains with)
Tutors (trains)

Clothed (dressed, attired)
Dressed (clothed)
Groomed (attired)

Fussy (particular)
Critical (fussy)
Complaining (critical)
Whining (complaining)

Petty (trivial)
Minor (petty)

Trivial (trifling)
Prepared (cooked)
Cooked (prepared)
Nutritious (nourishing)

Digestive (assimilative)
Intestinal (abdominal)

Clean (hygienic)
Sterile (clean)
Hygienic (clean)
Medicinal (hygienic)

Healing (curing)
Curable (treatable)
Health (therapy) Interests

Sick (in poor health)
Ill (sick)
Contagious (infectious)

83 **Virgo Adjective** Theme Words Listed Alphabetically

Accurate (factual)
Aiding (assisting)
Aligned (neat)
Attentive (faithful)
Attired (dressed)
Blessed (sainted)
Celibate (chaste)
Ceremonial (formal)
Certified (authentic)
Chaste (virginal)
Classifies (organizes)
Clean (hygienic)
Clear (explicit)
Clothed (dressed)
Complaining (critical)
Component (part of)
Constructive (helpful)
Contagious (infectious)
Cooked (prepared)
Correct (genuine)
Critical (fussy)
Curable (treatable)
Devoted (attentive)
Digestive (assimilative)
Discriminates (distinguishes)
Distinct (clear)
Dressed (clothed)
Dutiful (conscientious)
Equips (furnishes)

Exact (factual)
Exacting (painstaking)
Explicit (clear)
Factual (faithful to)
Faithful (dutiful)
Fastidious (exacting)
Formal (proper)
Fractional (partial)
Furnishes (provides)
Fussy (particular)
Genuine (legal or real)
Groomed (attired)
Healing (curing)
Health (therapy) Interests
Helpful (aiding)
Holy (pious)
Hygienic (clean)
Ill (sick)
Innocent (virtuous)
Intestinal (abdominal)
Itemizes (lists)
Medicinal (hygienic)
Meticulous (exacting)
Minor (petty)
Modest (proper)
Neat (tidy)
Nutritious (nourishing)
Orderly (arranged)
Organizes (classifies)

Part of (component)
Petty (trivial)
Practices (trains)
Precise (explicit)
Prepared (cooked)
Proper (formal)
Religious (holy)
Saintly (pious)
Segment (portion)
Selective (fastidious)
Sick (in poor health)
Solemn (ceremonial)
Sterile (clean)

Stocks (furnishes)
Supplies (equips)
Supportive (helpful)
Tidy (neat or orderly)
Trains (practices)
Trivial (trifling)
Tutors (trains)
Unambiguous (explicit)
Unmarked (undefaced)
Uses (trains with)
Virtuous (chaste)
Whining (complaining)

Virgo (Noun)

♍

Virgo (Noun) Essence

Virgo nouns show concerns for duty and service. This involves being the helping entity to others, and performing whatever services are needed, even if these are not specifically spelled out or itemized. What kind of help or assistance? This depends on the nature of the situation unfolding, but as a Virgo noun agent one must be prepared to meet any contingency or need. Doing a favor, rendering assistance, giving a boost of confidence, helping another to get a leg up – these are all forms of assistance.

Strong impulses prevail to strictly following rules and practices while helping and assisting others in the normal flow of life. Also, setting up individual categories, each with their own distinctions, examining details carefully, and following established procedures and sequences – remain important. Virgo nouns bring on a fussiness and particularity. They may effect a shyness and posture meaning there is a lack of concern but this is misleading. Worrying and agonizing about everything remains a constant companion. There also usually is an interest in healing activities and diet.

Maintaining order and neatness remains important. The Virgo noun emphasis remains strong on arranging items into categories, providing systems of organization, and sticking to and cleaning up groupings of pieces or information. Along with this ordering and neatness thrust comes the need for maintaining cleanliness and perfection. Perfection in what way? To whose ideal? To whatever ideal that compliments and completes the intended order that needs to be recognized and upheld.

Virgo nouns want to break tasks down into manageable parts, organize the pieces and components that go into making up the whole, and ensure that all parts and tools are kept available. If there are some items lost, unserviceable, broken or missing, then providing for restoring those damaged to their ideal is called for. The whole and entirety must be maintained.

To achieve this measurement and evaluation come into play. This involves maintaining a sense of precision that ensures that a viable and complete end product is achieved.

23 **Virgo Noun** Themes Grouped
Compiled from a Base of about 916 Words

Service (help or assistance)
Helping (assisting)
Assistance (helping)
Duty (service)

Obedience (compliance)
Conformity (obedience)
Compliance (obedience)

Precision (accuracy)
Accuracy (precision)
Care (accuracy)
Perfection (precision)

Neatness (orderliness)
Orderliness (uniformity)
Cleanliness (neatness)
Sterilization (disinfection)

Category (grouping)
Arrangement (organization)
Organization (system or arrangement)

Component (fragment)
Portion (part or piece)
Fragment (portion)
Piece (component)

Example (sample)
Detail (feature)

Feature (characteristic)
Characteristic (feature)

Examination (scrutiny)
Evaluation (scrutiny)
Scrutiny (examination)
Review (second look)

Measuring (marking out)
Counting (enumeration)
Figuring (computation)

Adjustment (repair)
Modification (revision)
Correction (adjustment)

Provisions (supplies)
Equipment (apparatus or supplies)
Apparatus (equipment)

Procedure (individual steps)
Technique (procedure or routine)
Sequence (order)
Method (process)

Ceremony (ritual)
Ritual (ceremony)
Formality (custom)

Training (practice or drill)

Drill (practice)
Indoctrination (instruction)

Complaint (criticism)
Criticism (gripe)
Gripe (complaint)

Choosy (particular)
Picky (fussy)
Particular (picky)

Modesty (decentness)
Humility (humbleness)
Shyness (modesty)

Celibacy (self-restraint)
Virginity (chastity)
Innocence (purity)
Virtue (decency)

Worry (anxiety)
Anxiety (worry)
Uneasiness (disquiet)

Clothing (attire or outfit)
Attire (clothing)
Dress (attire or clothing)

Digestion (absorbing food)
Digestive Issues (distresses)
Illness (distress)

Remedial (curing)
Cures (remedial treatments)
Medical Interests (healing therapies)

Diet (nutritional regimen)
Nutrition (good eating habits)
Nourishment (foodstuffs)

79 **Virgo Noun** Theme Words Listed Alphabetically

Accuracy (precision)
Adjustment (repair)
Anxiety (worry)
Apparatus (equipment)
Arrangement (organization)
Assistance (helping)
Attire (clothing)
Care (accuracy)
Category (grouping)

Celibacy (self-restraint)
Ceremony (ritual)
Characteristic (feature)
Choosy (particular)
Cleanliness (neatness)
Clothing (attire or outfit)
Complaint (criticism)
Compliance (obedience)
Component (fragment)

Conformity (obedience)
Correction (adjustment)
Counting (enumeration)
Criticism (gripe)
Critique (criticism)
Cures (remedial treatments)
Detail (feature)
Diet (nutritional regimen)
Digestion (absorbing food)
Digestive Issues (distresses)
Distress (illness)
Dress (attire or clothing)
Drill (practice)
Duty (service)
Equipment (apparatus or supplies)
Evaluation (scrutiny)
Examination (scrutiny)
Example (sample)
Feature (characteristic)
Figuring (computation)
Formality (custom)
Fragment (portion)
Gripe (complaint)
Helping (assisting)
Humility (humbleness)
Illness (distress)
Indoctrination (instruction)
Innocence (purity)
Measuring (marking out)
Medical Interests (healing therapies)
Method (process)

Modesty (decentness)
Modification (revision)
Neatness (orderliness)
Nourishment (foodstuffs)
Nutrition (good eating habits)
Obedience (compliance)
Orderliness (uniformity)
Organization (system or arrangement)
Particular (picky)
Perfection (precision)
Picky (fussy)
Piece (component)
Portion (part or piece)
Precision (accuracy)
Procedure (individual steps)
Provisions (supplies)
Remedial (curing)
Review (second look)
Ritual (ceremony)
Scrutiny (examination)
Sequence (order)
Service (help or assistance)
Shyness (modesty)
Sterilization (disinfection)
Technique (procedure or routine)
Training (practice or drill)
Uneasiness (disquiet)
Virginity (chastity)
Virtue (decency)
Worry (anxiety)

For Notations

Libra

Rulers: Yang Psyche and Yin Venus

Libra (Adjective) Essence

Libra adjectives show a strong drive to approach life in a way that assures agreement, and that each party work side-by-side and as co-equals with all others involved. When an imbalance arises as matters unfold, when one party takes advantage of another party, then the Libra adjective energies can come forth to adjust and set matters back to where harmony reigns. Some accusations may need addressing, like grievances revealed that show one party or another had been taken advantage of and in a wrong way. When this happens the Libra adjective energies help ensure that the need for adjustment and balance among all people or issues involved are addressed.

The desire for having life's activities remain harmonious, equalized, balanced and yet retain a satisfying proportion is strong. Getting to agreement, seeing that there is benefit for all in transactions, and doing things jointly is preferred. Libra adjectives inspire good mediators, who can remain poised and mannerly. Libra adjectives prefer purity and clarity, although a quickness to level accusations and have favorites is there too.

Libra adjectives search for like-mindedness, for agreement, for an equality resulting in a balance such that all parties are eventually satisfied. Libra adjectives have need for doing things jointly, sharing, and working cooperatively. Getting to a balance, and receiving and seeking satisfaction though, can take a lot of work, probably some time too. Along the way there may be some ruffled feelings, but with persistence the Libra adjectives can help bring resolution and satisfaction to any differences.

In Libra adjectives impartiality reigns. What is fair for one side in a transaction, or an encounter, equally needs to be fair for the other side. Consideration on how this can be achieved may take some time, but the overall balance and harmony of life does need to be addressed and adjusted where necessary. When necessary mediation and arbitration can be brought into play. Aggrieved sides need to see that their point of view is equally addressed and their grievances compensated for.

26 **Libra Adjective** Themes Grouped
Compiled from a Base of about 776 Words

Matched (paired)
Alike (agreeing)
Complementary (paired)
Paired (matched)

Compatible (fits with)
Coequal (equivalent)
Fits with (harmonious)
Harmonious (agreeable)

Balanced (equalized)
Adjusts for (suits)
Equalized (compensated)
Compensating (equalized)

Parallel (side-by-side)
Proportionate (equivalent)
Relative (coequal)
Symmetrical (proportional)

Agreeing (concurring)
Concurring (agreeing)
Cooperative (mutual)
Like-Minded (agreeing)

Befitting (suitable)
Appropriate (suitable)
Decent (proper)
Proper (suitable)

Joint (shared)
Mutual (joint)
United (together)
Together (in unison)

Synchronized (in agreement)
Simultaneous (concurrent)
Concurrent (simultaneous)
Attuned (harmonized)

Fair (unbiased)
Equitable (fair)
Impartial (unbiased)
Nonpartisan (impartial)

Considers (deliberates over)
Indecisive (wavering)
Undecided (vacillating)
Ambivalent (undecided)

Mediates (arbitrates)
Intercedes (mediates)
Decides (determines)
Settles (resolves)

Amidst (between)
Between (amidst)
Interposed (among)

Preferred (favored)
Favored (chosen)
Select (exclusive)
Exclusive (preferred)

Poised (dignified)
Refined (cultivated)
Mannerly (polite)
Civil (polite)

Divided (shared)
Halved (divided)
Shared (divided)

Inverse (transposed)
Transposed (inverted)
Reverse (inverse)
Contrasted to (opposite)

Debatable (questionable)
Controversial (debatable)
Disputable (debatable)

Disagreeing (at variance)
Alienated (opposed)
At Issue (opposed)
Opposed (contradicting)

Dissimilar (incompatible)
Incompatible (unsuited)
Unsuited (mismatched)
Mismatched (unsuited)

Accuses (implicates)
Incriminates (implicates)
Implicates (incriminates)

Liable (at fault)
Indefensible (beyond reason)
Accountable (beholden)
At fault (liable)

Bridal (nuptial)
Marital (conjugal)
Nuptial (wedding)

Pure (unmarked or clean)
Unmarked (unblemished)
Clean (unmarked)
Pristine (unused)

Clear (transparent)
Transparent (clear or see-through)
White (colorless)
Neutral (colorless)

Pale (washed out)
Ashen (pale)
Washed Out (blanched)

Spotted (mottled)
Speckled (spotted)
Multi-Hued (multi-colored)

97 **Libra Adjective** Theme Words Listed Alphabetically

Accountable (beholden)
Accuses (implicates)
Adjusts for (suits)
Agreeing (concurring)
Alienated (opposed)
Alike (agreeing)
Ambivalent (undecided)
Amidst (between)
Appropriate (suitable)
Ashen (pale)
At Issue (opposed)
At fault (liable)
Attuned (harmonized)
Balanced (equalized)
Befitting (suitable)
Between (amidst)
Bridal (nuptial)
Civil (polite)
Clean (unmarked)
Clear (transparent)
Coequal (equivalent)
Compatible (fits with)
Compensating (equalized)
Complementary (paired)
Concurrent (simultaneous)
Concurring (agreeing)
Considers (deliberates over)
Contrasted to (opposite)
Controversial (debatable)

Cooperative (mutual)
Debatable (questionable)
Decent (proper)
Decides (determines)
Disagreeing (at variance)
Disputable (debatable)
Dissimilar (incompatible)
Divided (shared)
Equalized (compensated)
Equitable (fair)
Exclusive (preferred)
Fair (unbiased)
Favored (chosen)
Fits with (harmonious)
Halved (divided)
Harmonious (agreeable)
Impartial (unbiased)
Implicates (incriminates)
Incompatible (unsuited)
Incriminates (implicates)
Indecisive (wavering)
Indefensible (beyond reason)
Intercedes (mediates)
Interposed (among)
Inverse (transposed)
Joint (shared)
Liable (at fault)
Like-Minded (agreeing)
Mannerly (polite)

Marital (conjugal)
Matched (paired)
Mediates (arbitrates)
Mismatched (unsuited)
Multi-Hued (multi-colored)
Mutual (joint)
Neutral (colorless)
Nonpartisan (impartial)
Nuptial (wedding)
Opposed (contradicting)
Paired (matched)
Pale (washed out)
Parallel (side-by-side)
Poised (dignified)
Preferred (favored)
Pristine (unused)
Proper (suitable)
Proportionate (equivalent)
Pure (unmarked or clean)
Refined (cultivated)

Relative (coequal)
Reverse (inverse)
Select (exclusive)
Settles (resolves)
Shared (divided)
Simultaneous (concurrent)
Speckled (spotted)
Spotted (mottled)
Symmetrical (proportional)
Synchronized (in agreement)
Together (in unison)
Transparent (clear or see-through)
Transposed (inverted)
Undecided (vacillating)
United (together)
Unmarked (unblemished)
Unsuited (mismatched)
Washed Out (blanched)
White (colorless)

Libra (Noun)

♎

Libra (Noun) Essence

An important highlight among the Libra noun energies involves reaching agreement and having assent. Along with this goes compromise and accommodation. What this implies is that seeking agreement, and working out of differences to each side's satisfaction remains an important part of Libra nouns. The need to find a common ground, the need to work out differences, and the need to pull together in a teamwork fashion are highlighted here. There cannot be an equality of partnership without agreement and compromise. When properly reached this can lead to peace and harmony amongst the parties involved.

Social action and activities retain a strong emphasis, and sometimes choosing among options can be difficult, as all appear to offer equal importance. Libra nouns want alternatives and choices among options to achieve a balance and harmony, to be in agreement. The legality and fairness of events in life play an important role. There can be many complaints received, and a separation or divorce among parties is possible if views and attitudes cannot be reconciled.

Equality is not the same as sameness. Equality implies that there is a balance, a uniformity in commitment to action and to status. Sameness implies that there is an oneness, where one is one way, and the other side is exactly mirrored in the same way and with the identical options and attributes. Sameness does not imply monotony, but it can lead to a lack of variety. Such lack is not what is called for here. Within equality there can be a harmony of expression where each side enforces the allure of the other in a reciprocal fashion. Uniformity can also be a desired goal.

Libra nouns call for social interaction and the correct social behavior. There are always alternatives and differences available, subtle as some may be, to lend shades of difference, contrasts to how matters appear to others. Sometimes it is exactly these subtle differences that help make acceptance and compliance achieve the desired equal ground of consensus.

24 **Libra Noun** Themes Grouped
Compiled from a Base of about 606 Words

Agreement (acknowledgment)
Acknowledgment (assent)
Assent (agreement)
Peace (harmony)

Compromise (accommodation)
Accommodation (compromise)
Harmony (consensus)
Adjustment (compromise)

Partnership (teaming)
Cooperation (teamwork)
Teamwork (cooperation)
Pulling Together (teamwork)

Clarity (unambiguity)
Transparency (clearness)
Unambiguity (clarity)

Balance (equilibrium)
Equilibrium (equality)
Stabilization (equilibrium)
Neutrality (impartiality)

Parity (equality)
Symmetry (uniformity)
Oneness (sameness)
Equality (parity)

Likeness (sameness)
Consistency (uniformity)
Conformity (consistency)
Matched (uniformity)

Relevance (aptness)
Applicability (relevance)
Suitability (relevance)

Legality (legitimacy)
Fairness (evenhandedness)
Rightfulness (legality)

Finesse (discretion)
Poise (composure)
Refinement (tastefulness)
Culture (intellectual taste)

Social Interaction (social engagement)
Hospitality (sociability)
Social Behavior (propriety)

Correlation (comparison)
Comparison (correlation)
Counterpart (opposite number)

Mediation (arbitration)
Intercession (intervention)
Negotiation (arbitration)
Alternative (another)

Contrast (difference)
Choice (alternative)
Option (alternative)

Weighing (considering)
Indecision (wavering)
Vacillation (ambivalence)

Contradiction (opposing statement)
Inequality (unfairness)
Inconsistency (discrepancy)

Opposite (inverse)
Inversion (reversal)
Reversal (transposition)

Rivalry (competitiveness)
Challenge (rivalry)
Competition (rivalry)

Conflict (clash of ideas)
Disagreement (dispute)

Confrontation (clash)
Dispute (altercation)

Complaint (accusation)
Accusation (complaint)
Misconception (misjudgment)
Objection (complaint)

Divorce (separation)
Break-Up (separation)
Separation (breaking-up)

Formal Union (marriage)
Marriage (merger)
Betrothal (proposal of marriage)

Purity (sanitizing)
Cleanliness (purity)

Paleness (wanness)
Lightness (paleness)

80 Libra Noun Theme Words Listed Alphabetically

Accommodation (compromise)
Accusation (complaint)
Acknowledgment (assent)
Adjustment (compromise)
Agreement (acknowledgment)
Alternative (another)
Applicability (relevance)
Assent (agreement)
Balance (equilibrium)
Betrothal (proposal of marriage)
Break-Up (separation)
Challenge (rivalry)
Choice (alternative)
Clarity (unambiguity)
Cleanliness (purity)
Comparison (correlation)
Competition (rivalry)
Complaint (accusation)
Compromise (accommodation)
Conflict (clash of ideas)
Conformity (consistency)
Confrontation (clash)
Consistency (uniformity)
Contradiction (opposing statement)
Contrast (difference)
Cooperation (teamwork)
Correlation (comparison)
Counterpart (opposite number)
Culture (intellectual taste)

Disagreement (dispute)
Dispute (altercation)
Divorce (separation)
Equality (parity)
Equilibrium (equality)
Fairness (evenhandedness)
Finesse (discretion)
Formal Union (marriage)
Harmony (consensus)
Hospitality (sociability)
Inconsistency (discrepancy)
Indecision (wavering)
Inequality (unfairness)
Intercession (intervention)
Inversion (reversal)
Legality (legitimacy)
Lightness (paleness)
Likeness (sameness)
Marriage (merger)
Matched (uniformity)
Mediation (arbitration)
Misconception (misjudgment)
Negotiation (arbitration)
Neutrality (impartiality)
Objection (complaint)
Oneness (sameness)
Opposite (inverse)
Option (alternative)
Paleness (wanness)

Parity (equality)
Partnership (teaming)
Peace (harmony)
Poise (composure)
Pulling Together (teamwork)
Purity (sanitizing)
Refinement (tastefulness)
Relevance (aptness)
Reversal (transposition)
Rightfulness (legality)
Rivalry (competitiveness)
Separation (breaking-up)

Social Behavior (propriety)
Social Interaction (social engagement)
Stabilization (equilibrium)
Suitability (relevance)
Symmetry (uniformity)
Teamwork (cooperation)
Transparency (clearness)
Unambiguity (clarity)
Vacillation (ambivalence)
Weighing (considering)

Scorpio

♏

Rulers: Yang Pluto and Yin Mars

Scorpio (Adjective) Essence

Within Scorpio adjectives lies an intention, a deliberate and purposeful manner, to whatever is chosen. Scorpio adjectives show consideration and thoughtfulness. But Scorpio adjectives will tend toward what they feel is in their best interests. Usually there can be a deliberately calculated and internally devised reason with their approaches and methods. They usually weigh each decision carefully; even those made quickly, and rarely make any commitment or movement without having a deliberate purpose in mind.

The focus here comes with a determination and a purpose to all that is considered or attempted. Scorpio adjectives bring strong fixations on their ideas and approaches. Yet they can also have remaining doubts and remain suspicious. If there is an action or idea that is contrary to their way then they may work to suppress that. Being vindictive and spiteful may also be their way. They remain cunning and secretive, and prefer hidden agendas.

Scorpio adjective energies can take on an issue or a topic and become completely absorbed in that. They are capable of bringing an intense concentration to the moment, even to the exclusion of any other impulse or stimulus that would detract their attention away from what they are currently focused upon. They can retain a razor-sharp focus on what they feel is needed to hold their attention, and other impulses, other distractions, are usually ignored while they internally process out the effect that their current focus of concentration is liable to have on other forces.

Doubt and suspicion about motives or intentions can remain, but when these have been resolved then the Scorpio adjective loyalty to what has been accepted should remain unquestioned. Scorpio adjectives may appear hesitant or leery about approaching a subject or a person, but as they go through their internal analysis to determine if there is safety, then upon resolution and acceptance a tremendous amount of trust is put in place. Scorpio adjectives bring on the makings of a good analyst, detective, etc.

20 **Scorpio Adjective** Themes Grouped
Compiled from a Base of about 693 Words

Determined (willful)
Purposeful (deliberate)
Deliberate (intended)
Willful (deliberate)

Absorbed (obsessed)
Preoccupied (absorbed with)
Intense (consuming)
Obsessed with (controlled by)

Analyzes (examines)
Examines (studies)
Thorough (particular)
Penetrating (incisive)

Doubtful (skeptical)
Suspicious (mistrustful)
Skeptical (doubting)
Leery (distrustful)

Controls (manipulates)
Oppresses (subjugates)
Influences (controls)
Regulates (controls)

Domineering (intimidating)
Dictatorial (domineering)
Tyrannical (dictatorial)
Bossy (domineering)

Forced (compelled)
Compelled (pressed)
Compulsory (forced)
Requires (obligates)

Confirms (establishes)
Verifies (substantiates)
Sanctions (confirms)
Permits (allows)

Disciplines (chastises)
Scolds (chides)
Reprimands (scolds)
Chides (scolds)

Refrains from (avoids)
Renounces (repudiates)
Suppresses (restrains)
Foregoes (gives up)

Denies (rejects)
Never (not ever)
Represses (shuts in)
Rejects (declines)

Exempted (immune)
Immune (spared)
Protected (preserved)
Spared (exempted)

Unfaithful (disloyal)
Heretical (unbelieving)
Pagan (atheistic)
Irreligious (irreverent)

Obligated (duty bound)
Binding (obligated)
Indebted (obligated)
Committed (obligated)

Vindictive (vengeful)
Revengeful (vindictive)
Spiteful (revengeful)
Reciprocates (retaliates)

Compacted (dense)
Dense (compact)
Concentrated (dense)

Corrupt (depraved)
Unethical (immoral)
Perverted (kinky)
Illicit (illegal)

Cunning (devious)
Sneaky (secretive)
Devious (sneaky)
Sly (devious)

Secretive (hidden)
Hidden (secretive)
Esoteric (secret)
Private (nonpublic)

Unknowable (baffling)
Puzzling (baffling)
Elusive (baffling)
Enigmatic (puzzling)

79 **Scorpio Adjective** Theme Words Listed Alphabetically

Absorbed (obsessed)
Analyzes (examines)
Binding (obligated)
Bossy (domineering)
Chides (scolds)
Committed (obligated)
Compacted (dense)
Compelled (pressed)
Compulsory (forced)
Concentrated (dense)
Confirms (establishes)
Controls (manipulates)
Corrupt (depraved)
Cunning (devious)
Deliberate (intended)
Denies (rejects)
Dense (compact)
Determined (willful)
Devious (sneaky)
Dictatorial (domineering)
Disciplines (chastises)
Domineering (intimidating)
Doubtful (skeptical)
Elusive (baffling)
Enigmatic (puzzling)
Esoteric (secret)
Examines (studies)
Exempted (immune)
Forced (compelled)

Foregoes (gives up)
Heretical (unbelieving)
Hidden (secretive)
Illicit (illegal)
Immune (spared)
Indebted (obligated)
Influences (controls)
Intense (consuming)
Irreligious (irreverent)
Leery (distrustful)
Never (not ever)
Obligated (duty bound)
Obsessed with (controlled by)
Oppresses (subjugates)
Pagan (atheistic)
Penetrating (incisive)
Permits (allows)
Perverted (kinky)
Preoccupied (absorbed with)
Private (nonpublic)
Protected (preserved)
Purposeful (deliberate)
Puzzling (baffling)
Reciprocates (retaliates)
Refrains from (avoids)
Regulates (controls)
Rejects (declines)
Renounces (repudiates)
Represses (shuts in)

Reprimands (scolds)
Requires (obligates)
Revengeful (vindictive)
Sanctions (confirms)
Scolds (chides)
Secretive (hidden)
Skeptical (doubting)
Sly (devious)
Sneaky (secretive)
Spared (exempted)
Spiteful (revengeful)

Suppresses (restrains)
Suspicious (mistrustful)
Thorough (particular)
Tyrannical (dictatorial)
Unethical (immoral)
Unfaithful (disloyal)
Unknowable (baffling)
Verifies (substantiates)
Vindictive (vengeful)
Willful (deliberate)

Rulers: Yang Pluto and Yin Mars

Scorpio (Noun)

♏

Scorpio (Noun) Essence

Scorpio nouns bring a willful determination to get to the essence or truth behind issues. At the core here is getting to and understanding the central principles of what lies behind an idea or activity. For those not able to see the Scorpio noun interpretation or point of view the energies here can resort to recrimination and reprimands. Scorpio nouns do not take well to others breaking established rules or customs. Occult and ritual magic practices bring an interest, as do puzzling or baffling situations.

When determining to make a commitment or pledge, Scorpio nouns can be all in for the duration. Their allegiance should not be questioned at this time. Yes, they may eventually have a change of mind; they may go off in other directions, but never without deep thought and a careful consideration of what the consequences can be for self and also upon others. Any change of direction after a commitment is made is usually based upon having been fooled or misled about the original intentions or promises. Hooked they can be, but should Scorpio nouns find out they have been misled or fooled, then their personal wrath can be unleashed in forceful ways.

Determination, steadfastness and loyalty remain important. Obtaining permission for what is intended is necessary. Scorpio nouns want to ensure that their consent is clearly given when called for. Setting a clarity of intention and a well-defined path can lessen their distrust and suspicions.

When the Scorpio noun intentions have been exploited, when their loyalty has been questioned, or actions they openly done are called into account or misrepresented, then a powerful internal urge to seek vengeance can come forth. There definitely is an 'eye for an eye' inner thrust here. Failure to meet an obligation or a promise can bring on retribution.

Privacy and confidentiality remain as important issues. When Scorpio nouns promise, or if are asked to keep the idea of another confidential, they are quite able to do so. Scorpio nouns can be stealthy, they can be revengeful, and they can expect reciprocal compensation for what has been done.

14 **Scorpio Noun** Themes Grouped
Compiled from a Base of about 442 Words

Commitment (pledge)
Assurance (commitment)
Allegiance (commitment)
Pledge (promise)

Control (enforcement)
Enforcement (crackdown)
Regulations (rules)
Rule (criterion)

Focus (preoccupation)
Fixation (obsession)
Single-Mindedness (fixation)
Obsession (absorption)

Study (investigation)
Analysis (study)
Interpretation (explanation)
Investigation (probing)

Determination (findings)
Findings (determinations)
Research (investigation)
Inquiry (investigation)

Permission (consent)
Authorization (permission)
Consent (privilege)
License (permission)

Mistrust (skepticism)
Suspicion (doubt)
Resentment (mistrust)
Skepticism (doubt)

Admonishment (scolding)
Scolding (reprimand)
Reprimand (berating)
Rebuke (censure or scolding)

Infidelity (breach of vows)
Betrayal (breach of faith)
Disloyalty (unfaithfulness)
Treachery (betrayal)

Restitution (repayment)
Obligation (pledge)
Repayment (redress or amends)
Amends (compensation)

Revenge (vindication)
Vindication (justification)
Reciprocity (interplay)
Retaliation (retribution)

Privacy (secrecy)
Confidentiality (privacy)
Secrecy (privacy)
Stealth (secrecy)

Occult (the supernatural)
Supernatural (the occult)
Magic (sorcery)
Sorcery (witchcraft)

Baffling (puzzling)
Enigma (puzzle)
Cryptic (inscrutable)
Intrigue (mystery)

56 **Scorpio Noun** Theme Words Listed Alphabetically

Admonishment (scolding)
Allegiance (commitment)
Amends (compensation)
Analysis (study)
Assurance (commitment)
Authorization (permission)
Baffling (puzzling)
Betrayal (breach of faith)
Commitment (pledge)
Confidentiality (privacy)
Consent (privilege)
Control (enforcement)
Cryptic (inscrutable)
Determination (findings)
Disloyalty (unfaithfulness)
Enforcement (crackdown)
Enigma (puzzle)
Findings (determinations)
Fixation (obsession)
Focus (preoccupation)
Infidelity (breach of vows)
Inquiry (investigation)
Interpretation (explanation)

Intrigue (mystery)
Investigation (probing)
License (permission)
Magic (sorcery)
Mistrust (skepticism)
Obligation (pledge)
Obsession (absorption)
Occult (the supernatural)
Permission (consent)
Pledge (promise)
Privacy (secrecy)
Rebuke (censure or scolding)
Reciprocity (interplay)
Regulations (rules)
Repayment (redress or amends)
Reprimand (berating)
Research (investigation)
Resentment (mistrust)
Restitution (repayment)
Retaliation (retribution)
Revenge (vindication)
Rule (criterion)
Scolding (reprimand)

Secrecy (privacy)
Single-Mindedness (fixation)
Skepticism (doubt)
Sorcery (witchcraft)
Stealth (secrecy)

Study (investigation)
Supernatural (the occult)
Suspicion (doubt)
Treachery (betrayal)
Vindication (justification)

For Notations

Sagittarius

Rulers: Yang Neptune and Yin Jupiter

Sagittarius (Adjective) Essence

The Sagittarius adjective emphasis lies on being comprehensive, taking an all-inclusive view of ongoing events and circumstances, and then trying to put such into a broader context that can place perspective on life unfolding. Nothing small here, no minor details, just the big picture view, and how this can answer the overall questions of "who", "what", "why" and "where" that keep popping up. Sagittarius adjectives bring demands for answers, for understanding, the overall context, for placing perspective on happenings. The Sagittarius adjectives focus on providing a context, an understanding, for addressing matters.

The Sagittarius adjective emphasis is on an ability to see "the big picture"; an overview of events and circumstances that helps put matters into a context for understanding. Acceptable are theories, speculations, assumptions, approximations, and even if things are a bit "off the mark" that too is tolerable. An unhampered approach, being open and direct, is called for and what is taken.

Sagittarius adjectives prefer the broad overview, and assumptions are allowed. Approximations can be made, and if a "guess" can be good enough to satisfy a curiosity, then that too is acceptable. No pinpointing to the details, no taking task to find the absolute truth, just getting close enough to satisfy inquiry is what is addressed here. Devising, guessing at, making approximations, and even inventing answers based on assumptions can become acceptable.

Such attitudes for "just good enough" can lead to unintended consequences. Inadvertent comments may lead to misunderstandings, but then the idealistic nature of the justifications can turn inquires into acceptable answers. Hints that such is correct, exaggerations of tales leading to or mirroring myths, the exploration of how and why things happened in the past, and how they have shaped present reality come into play here.

The Sagittarian adjectives show a need for expanding knowledge, gaining insight through education, and opening new paths for better understanding.

21 **Sagittarius Adjective** Themes Grouped
Compiled from a Base of about 814 Words

Comprehensive (inclusive)
All-Inclusive (sweeping)
Panoramic (sweeping)
Sweeping (broad or extensive)

Far-Reaching (wide-ranging)
Widespread (extended)
Furthermost (uttermost)
Extensive (far-flung)

Theoretical (speculative)
Speculative (hypothetical)
Possible (likely)
Conjectural (theoretical)

Assumed (concocted)
Invented (fabricated)
Concocted (cooked up)
Devised (contrived)

Approximate (estimated)
Estimated (assumed)
Presumed (approximated)
Rough (guessed at)

Off-the-Mark (imprecise)
Inaccurate (imprecise)
Imprecise (inexact)
Astray (off-the-mark)

Exaggerated (overstated)
Embellished (added to)
Far-Fetched (exaggerated)
Stretched (enhanced)

Legendary (fabled)
Mythical (legendary)
Imaginary (hypothetical)
Allegorical (legendary)

Indirect (inferred)
Hinted (rumored)
Inferred (speculated)
Roundabout (indirect)

Candid (direct)
Frank (open or candid)
Outspoken (forthright)
Direct (forthright)

Unscheduled (unintended)
Inadvertent (unintended)
Unintentional (inadvertent)
Uncommitted (unplanned)

Unarranged (thrown together)
Thrown Together (slapdash)
Perfunctory (rushed through)
Hit-or-miss (accidental)

Idealistic (envisioned)
Liberal (idealistic)
Broad-Minded (idealistic)
Philosophical (envisioned)

Unhampered (unobstructed)
Unobstructed (clear)
Unblocked (unobstructed)
Exposed (unobstructed)

Folksy (informal)
Informal (casual)
Casual (informal)
Easygoing (informal)

Digressive (rambling)
Rambling (discursive)
Verbose (wordy)
Long-Winded (verbose)

Schooled (learned)

Educated (learned)
Well-Versed (scholarly)
Learned (academic)

Distant (remote)
Remote (distant)
Foreign (not native)
Exotic (foreign)

Footloose (venturesome)
Adventurous (footloose)
Leave-Taking (departing)

Religious (theological)
Liturgical (ceremonial)
Ministerial (ecclesiastical)
Churchy (religious)

Anthropomorphic (human shaped)

80 **Sagittarius Adjective** Theme Words Listed Alphabetically

Adventurous (footloose)
All-Inclusive (sweeping)
Allegorical (legendary)
Anthropomorphic (human shaped)
Approximate (estimated)
Assumed (concocted)
Astray (off-the-mark)
Broad-Minded (idealistic)
Candid (direct)
Casual (informal)
Churchy (religious)
Comprehensive (inclusive)
Concocted (cooked up)
Conjectural (theoretical)
Devised (contrived)
Digressive (rambling)
Direct (forthright)
Distant (remote)
Easygoing (informal)
Educated (learned)
Embellished (added to)
Estimated (assumed)
Exaggerated (overstated)
Exotic (foreign)
Exposed (unobstructed)
Extensive (far-flung)
Far-Fetched (exaggerated)
Far-Reaching (wide-ranging)
Folksy (informal)

Footloose (venturesome)
Foreign (not native)
Frank (open or candid)
Furthermost (uttermost)
Hinted (rumored)
Hit-or-Miss (accidental)
Idealistic (envisioned)
Imaginary (hypothetical)
Imprecise (inexact)
Inaccurate (imprecise)
Inadvertent (unintended)
Indirect (inferred)
Inferred (speculated)
Informal (casual)
Invented (fabricated)
Learned (academic)
Leave-Taking (departing)
Legendary (fabled)
Liberal (idealistic)
Liturgical (ceremonial)
Long-Winded (verbose)
Ministerial (ecclesiastical)
Mythical (legendary)
Off-the-Mark (imprecise)
Outspoken (forthright)
Panoramic (sweeping)
Perfunctory (rushed through)
Philosophical (envisioned)
Possible (likely)

Presumed (approximated)
Rambling (discursive)
Religious (theological)
Remote (distant)
Rough (guessed at)
Roundabout (indirect)
Schooled (learned)
Speculative (hypothetical)
Stretched (enhanced)
Sweeping (broad or extensive)
Theoretical (speculative)
Thrown Together (slapdash)

Unarranged (thrown together)
Unblocked (unobstructed)
Uncommitted (unplanned)
Unhampered (unobstructed)
Unintentional (inadvertent)
Unobstructed (clear)
Unscheduled (unintended)
Verbose (wordy)
Well-Versed (scholarly)
Widespread (extended)

Sagittarius (Noun)

Sagittarius (Noun) Essence

Within the Sagittarius noun arena there is nothing like proposing a new assumption, a theory, a hypothesis, and then stretching, refining and expanding on that in any one of a thousand ways. The mindboggling possibilities for speculation seem to be endless, and almost like a game of exploration within the mind, and they can go on and on. How many assumptions can be made about how the theory can expand or be applied? What is the premise behind each such assumption? Can a guess be taken? These can be seen as Sagittarius nouns working at their best.

Justifications for the theoretical approach, seeing the "broad picture", and stating conjectures or alternatives to what is already known, remain strong. There are schemes and bluffs and tactics, each justified by ramblings and ambiguities. It is hard to keep still as there needs to be much jumping around, leading to distractions and inattention. The end result can be an adventure that satisfies the Sagittarius nouns need to wander.

If the words "assume that … " come up in a conversation, then this may be the result of a Sagittarius noun influence. Especially if that is followed by an overview of possibilities, the mention of getting a "rough idea", making an assumption about possibilities or outcome, etc. These may be used along with analogies, hypotheses, or impressions. Nothing concrete or down to earth is offered, just material to exercise judgment. Helping this is the tendency to digress, and to get into endless long-winded explanations.

Addressing first one subject, then another, or just jumping over the hurdles of life come naturally. Intruding thoughts can lead to daydreaming about possibilities, or bring distractions and inattention to matters that needing better focus and attention. There is a need here for exploration, along with an internal need where the chase is preferred to the capture.

The Sagittarius noun focus includes a naturalness, an informality, as well as an openness and frankness of expression. Before they know it words that can hurt or sting others are out of their mouths, and there is no taking those back without making serious amends.

15 **Sagittarius Noun** Themes Grouped
Compiled from a Base of about 515 Words

Concept (idea)
Theory (hypothesis)
Hunch (impression)
Premise (assumption)
Hypothesis (supposition)

Analogy (comparison)
Correlation (analogy)
Comparison (analogy)

Elaboration (expansion)
Clarification (excuse)
Justification (rationalization)
Excuse (justification)

Estimation (guess)
Assumption (guess)
Guess (estimate)
Conjecture (speculation)
Opinion (point of view)

Broad Picture (overview)
Overview (broad picture)
Perspective (big picture)
Rough Idea (overview)

Scheme (stratagem)
Tactic (plot or strategy)
Bluff (open deception)

Concoction (fabrication)
Stunt (feat or trick)

Digression (long-windedness)
Ramblings (digressions)
Verbosity (wordiness)
Long-Windedness (verbosity)

Exaggeration (overstatement)
Overstatement (embellishment)
Vagueness (generality)
Ambiguity (vagueness)

Symbol (metaphor)
Myth (legend)
Allegory (myth)
Proverb (adage)

Exploration (adventure)
Adventure (exploration)
Chase the (pursuit as in a game)
Unfettered (freedom loving)
Wanderlust (need to roam)

Jumping (leaping)
Hurdling (leaping over)
Leaping (vaulting)
Crossing Over (clearing)

Informality (naturalness)
Candidness (directness)
Frankness (openness)
Sincerity (earnestness)

Inattention (oversight)

Error in Judgment (absentmindedness)
Preoccupation (daydreaming)
Absentmindedness (inattention)

Anthropomorphism

Pointed Objects (e.g., needles, scissors)

57 **Sagittarius Noun** Theme Words Listed Alphabetically

Absentmindedness (inattention)
Adventure (exploration)
Allegory (myth)
Ambiguity (vagueness)
Analogy (comparison)
Anthropomorphism
Assumption (guess)
Bluff (open deception)
Broad Picture (overview)
Candidness (directness)
Chase the (pursuit as in a game)
Clarification (excuse)
Comparison (analogy)
Concept (idea)
Concoction (fabrication)
Conjecture (speculation)
Correlation (analogy)
Crossing Over (clearing)

Digression (long-windedness)
Elaboration (expansion)
Error in Judgment (absentmindedness)
Estimation (guess)
Exaggeration (overstatement)
Excuse (justification)
Exploration (adventure)
Frankness (openness)
Guess (estimate)
Hunch (impression)
Hurdling (leaping over)
Hypothesis (supposition)
Inattention (oversight)
Informality (naturalness)
Jumping (leaping)
Justification (rationalization)
Leaping (vaulting)
Long-Windedness (verbosity)

Myth (legend)

Opinion (point of view)

Overstatement (embellishment)

Overview (broad picture)

Perspective (big picture)

Pointed Objects (e.g., needles, scissors)

Premise (assumption)

Preoccupation (daydreaming)

Proverb (adage)

Ramblings (digressions)

Rough Idea (overview)

Scheme (stratagem)

Sincerity (earnestness)

Stunt (feat or trick)

Symbol (metaphor)

Tactic (plot or strategy)

Theory (hypothesis)

Unfettered (freedom loving)

Vagueness (generality)

Verbosity (wordiness)

Wanderlust (need to roam)

For Notations

Capricorn

♑

Rulers: Yang Uranus and Yin Saturn

Capricorn (Adjective) Essence

For the Capricorn adjectives sticking to a goal, completing a task, and seeing matters underway through to the end remain a central part. Capricorn adjectives help with the assessment of how much the personal resources of time and energy an assignment should occupy. The idea of sticking matters through to completion, and not giving up despite obstacles encountered, or blockages along the path of completion, are shown here.

An overwhelming ambition to move ahead despite obstacles is followed on with a persistent and systematic approach. Capricorn adjectives plan for and prepare in thorough ways to find what works, and what the most practical or functional outcome can be. Uniformity and consistency mirror their business-like approach. Capricorn adjectives show an honesty and morality, but also a sense of caution, even thriftiness.

Capricorn adjectives with their need for thorough planning bring a good grasp on what resources are needed to begin. Review the steps of a procedure from start to finish, then check back to ensure nothing important has been overlooked, and then follow the plan of attack from start to finish. Good planning implies thorough preparation. Thorough preparation implies a sensible approach and a practical look at whether the resources needed to undertake and complete a task are worth the end product.

Capricorn adjectives bring an emphasis on the practical and useful side of approaching a task. Questions like: Is this undertaking suitable for the resources and time needed to commit to it? Has too much or too little been taken on? The Capricorn adjective words show a focus on using the present resources of time and energy correctly, thoroughly and effectively.

The Capricorn adjective words focus on a business-like approach. Being accountable for one's action or intentions is a major part of their plan.

22 **Capricorn Adjective** Themes Grouped
Compiled from a Base of about 709 Words

Persistent (tenacious)
Diligent (persistent)
Systematic (methodical)
Prevails (determined)

Ambitious (enterprising)
Industrious (hard-working)
Occupied (busy)
Busy (occupied)

Dependable (prompt)
Reliable (trusty)
Sensible (prudent)
Prompt (on time)

Thorough (conscientious)
Meticulous (thorough)
Exhaustive (painstaking)
Technical (methodical)

Plans for (schedules)
Prepared (ready)
Schedules (prepares)
Ready (prepared)

Qualified (eligible)
Experienced (qualified)
Skilled (proficient)
Capable (qualified)

Effective (working)
Functional (working)
Working (operative)
Tested (tried)

Practical (useful)
Useful (functional or helpful)
Productive (useful)
Expedient (useful)

Suitable (appropriate)
Pertinent (germane)
Fitting (appropriate)
Appropriate (befitting)

Uniform (consistent)
Consistent (regular)
Regular (uniform or orderly)
Orderly (regular)

Attainable (reachable)
Reachable (attainable)
Possible (attainable)

Laborious (strenuous)
Toilsome (laborious)
Strenuous (laborious)
Arduous (demanding)

Businesslike (practical)
Manageable (teachable)
Governable (controllable)

Administrative (organized)
Organized (standardized)
Managing (administering)

Official (authorized)
Authoritative (official)
Sanctioned (authorized)
Approved (official)

Principled (law-abiding)
Ethical (honest)
Honest (aboveboard)
Proper (ethical)

Accountable (responsible)
Responsible (answerable)
Liable (answerable)

Withdrawn (distant)
Unresponsive (reserved)

Reserved (withdrawn)
Formal (reserved)

Stern (strict or demanding)
Strict (merciless)
Pitiless (hard-hearted)
Demanding (stern)

Wary (cautious)
Careful (cautious)
Cautious (prudent)
Reluctant (hesitant)

Thrifty (frugal)
Economical (thrifty)
Cheap (economical)

Leathery (like leather)
Reptilian (leathery)

81 **Capricorn Adjective** Theme Words Listed Alphabetically

Accountable (responsible)
Administrative (organized)
Ambitious (enterprising)
Approved (official)
Appropriate (befitting)
Arduous (demanding)
Attainable (reachable)
Authoritative (official)
Businesslike (practical)
Busy (occupied)

Capable (qualified)
Careful (cautious)
Cautious (prudent)
Cheap (economical)
Consistent (regular)
Demanding (stern)
Dependable (prompt)
Diligent (persistent)
Economical (thrifty)
Effective (working)

Ethical (honest)
Exhaustive (painstaking)
Expedient (useful)
Experienced (qualified)
Fitting (appropriate)
Formal (reserved)
Functional (working)
Governable (controllable)
Honest (aboveboard)
Industrious (hard-working)
Laborious (strenuous)
Leathery (like leather)
Liable (answerable)
Manageable (teachable)
Managing (administering)
Meticulous (thorough)
Occupied (busy)
Official (authorized)
Orderly (regular)
Organized (standardized)
Persistent (tenacious)
Pertinent (germane)
Pitiless (hard-hearted)
Plans for (schedules)
Possible (attainable)
Practical (useful)
Prepared (ready)
Prevails (determined)
Principled (law-abiding)
Productive (useful)
Prompt (on time)

Proper (ethical)
Qualified (eligible)
Reachable (attainable)
Ready (prepared)
Regular (uniform or orderly)
Reliable (trusty)
Reluctant (hesitant)
Reptilian (leathery)
Reserved (withdrawn)
Responsible (answerable)
Sanctioned (authorized)
Schedules (prepares)
Sensible (prudent)
Skilled (proficient)
Stern (strict or demanding)
Strenuous (laborious)
Strict (merciless)
Suitable (appropriate)
Systematic (methodical)
Technical (methodical)
Tested (tried)
Thorough (conscientious)
Thrifty (frugal)
Toilsome (laborious)
Uniform (consistent)
Unresponsive (reserved)
Useful (functional or helpful)
Wary (cautious)
Withdrawn (distant)
Working (operative)

Capricorn (Noun)

♑

Capricorn (Noun) Essence

A strong focus within Capricorn nouns lies with taking obligation for managing ongoing efforts seriously. Execution and overall competence remain important. Retaining supervision over all aspects of any ongoing efforts made takes on an urgency. This involves ensuring that attention remains focused and good communication exists among all parts and those involved. Having good administrators, or even ensuring that self does the administration over the various parts of any effort, shows strongly here.

Capricorn nouns take their responsibilities seriously, and feel that reputation should reflect and include a thorough and competent work ethic. Therefore careful preparation, setting standards, attaining accreditation, etc., become a part of life. They manage and issue instructions and guidelines that help ensure success. There is a reliance on making sure that matters in hand are done correctly. For Capricorn nouns ambition can provide a strong push. Yet stinginess with resources or affection may remain.

Good planning begins with good management and ensuring that ongoing supervision can monitor progress and movement along noted checkpoints is important. These checkpoints pave the way toward the desired outcome. Discipline needs to be maintained. The qualification of those involved or the quality of materials chosen need to match the standards set for meeting the desired end goals. There needs to be clear definitions for these checkpoints, each step distinguishing one from the other, with each step given a start and ending point.

What sets the definition of a project? What determines its purpose? This involves a clear understanding of what is expected at the end of any effort. There needs to be clarity of intention. Aims are set and goals are undertaken with a definite objective in mind. Capricorn nouns are about the execution of a plan so that intentions can be realized. Instructions and guidelines must remain clear, and ongoing directives cannot change much within ongoing progress without a redefinition of end goals. A project may be as simple as doing household laundry, or as complicated as building a car.

14 **Capricorn Noun** Themes Grouped
Compiled from a Base of about 498 Words

Responsibility (accountability)
Accountability (responsibility)
Obligation (responsibility)
Reliability (responsibility)

Management (administration)
Supervision (oversight)
Regulation (administration)
Administration (supervision)

Resoluteness (resolve)
Persistence (determination)
Determination (resolve)
Tenacity (persistence)

Execution (performance)
Performance (execution)
Competence (performance)
Ability (competence)

Usefulness (functionality)
Applicability (properness)
Suitability (aptness)
Aptness (usefulness)

Qualifications (certification)
Certification (accreditation)
Accreditation (standards)
Standards (criteria)

Occupation (business)
Position (function or occupation)
Livelihood (occupation)
Function (purpose)

Preparation (plan)
Making Ready (preparation)
Readiness (preparedness)
Planning (scheduling)

Instructions (guidelines)
Guidance (instruction)
Directives (orders)
Standards (instructions)

Intention (purpose)
Undertaking (project)
Aim (intention)
Plan (objective)

Ambition (initiative)
Initiative (drive)
Boldness (initiative)
Aspiration (ambition)

Certainty (validity)
Actuality (certainty)
Validity (soundness)
Reliance (confidence)

Ascent (moving upwards)
Arising (ascending)
Moving Upwards (ascending)
Climbing (ascending)

Meagerness (stinginess)
Tight-Fistedness (stinginess)
Stinginess (cheapness)

55 **Capricorn Noun** Theme Words Listed Alphabetically

Ability (competence)
Accountability (responsibility)
Accreditation (standards)
Actuality (certainty)
Administration (supervision)
Aim (intention)
Ambition (initiative)
Applicability (properness)
Aptness (usefulness)
Arising (ascending)
Ascent (moving upwards)
Aspiration (ambition)
Boldness (initiative)
Certainty (validity)
Certification (accreditation)
Climbing (ascending)
Competence (performance)
Determination (resolve)
Directives (orders)
Execution (performance)
Function (purpose)
Guidance (instruction)

Initiative (drive)
Instructions (guidelines)
Intention (purpose)
Livelihood (occupation)
Making Ready (preparation)
Management (administration)
Meagerness (stinginess)
Moving Upwards (ascending)
Obligation (responsibility)
Occupation (business)
Performance (execution)
Persistence (determination)
Plan (objective)
Planning (scheduling)
Position (function or occupation)
Preparation (plan)
Qualifications (certification)
Readiness (preparedness)
Regulation (administration)
Reliability (responsibility)
Reliance (confidence)
Resoluteness (resolve)

Responsibility (accountability)
Standards (criteria)
Standards (instructions)
Stinginess (cheapness)
Suitability (aptness)
Supervision (oversight)

Tenacity (persistence)
Tight-Fistedness (stinginess)
Undertaking (project)
Usefulness (functionality)
Validity (soundness)

Aquarius

Rulers: Yang Saturn and Yin Uranus

Aquarius (Adjective) Essence

Aquarius adjectives place an emphasis on humanity, tolerance, and other-directedness toward friends and/or groups. This comes along with a personal detachment, and that can come through as non-involvement at an emotional level. Aquarius adjectives show a down-playing of personal ego, so that what results is a genuine interest in the affairs and concerns for and about others, but in a way that bypasses any emotional attachment levels. Bringing friends together, with an equal involvement for all, shows forth here. Aquarius adjectives show an ability to remain aloof and detached from ongoing situations, something that may be taken as insensitivity.

Aquarius adjectives bring a friendliness, even a genuine concern, but without getting into the emotional side that may imply a deeper commitment than what is intended. They prefer to keep matters impersonal, impassioned, and detached. Yes, a somewhat superficial interest in the welfare of others is shown, but a deeper personal attachment does not always come along with this. Keeping company and fellowship shine forth with befriending.

Fraternization while maintaining independence, showing a friendly and neighborly front, and invitations to join in with self and others reside here. There is a need to apportion, divide, and mix components. Interests in communal and joint activities remains strong, yet there is an aloof and unconcerned pallor that overrides many of such undertakings.

There is a need to mix, to blend, and to intermingle parts and pieces that are not always considered together. A drive for alternatives, assortments, and something that transcends categories remains. Setting a strict regimen? Following a prescribed course? Not here. More likely is an experiment, taking parts from this, and pieces from that, to produce something new that has not been brought about elsewhere. The idea of involvement in community, civic and/or municipal activities, of participating in civilized social interaction, but mostly at an impersonal level, remains high.

17 Aquarius Adjective Themes Grouped
Compiled from a Base of about 682 Words

Humanitarian (altruistic)
Altruistic (humanitarian)
Integrated (nonsectarian)
Tolerant (humanitarian)

Friendly (companionable)
Approachable (friendly)
Neighborly (friendly)
Open (accessible)

Fraternizes (mingles) with
Associates with (befriends)
Befriends (affiliates with)

Independent (separate from)
Individualistic (independent)
Original (independent)
Stands Apart (separate from)

Summons (invites)
Assembles (gathers together)
Invites (summons)
Calls (summons)

Impersonal (uninvolved)
Detached (cool or distant)
Clinical (impersonal)
Objective (impartial)

Mixes (combines)
Combines (blends)

Blends (combines)
Scrambles (mixes)

Divides (apportions)
Apportions (divides)
Allocates (dispenses)
Dispenses (disburses)

Scatters (strews)
Disperses (distributes)
Strews (throws around)
Circulates (scatters)

Assorted (diversified)
Diversified (varied)
Unique (distinct)
Different (unique)

Alternates (rotates)
Switches (varies)
Shifts (switches)
Rotates (switches)

Communal (common)
Civic (municipal)
Municipal (civic)
Political (civil)

Legislative (lawmaking)
Governmental (legislative)
Lawmaking (political)

Parliamentary (legislative)

Crowded (packed)
Full (filled)
Teeming (filled)
Crammed (congested)

Modern (contemporary)
Novel (new)
Contemporary (modern)
Progressive (trend-setting)

Aloof (reserved)
Reserved (indifferent)
Unconcerned (uninterested)
Removed (aloof)

Callous (insensitive)
Apathetic (callous)
Insensitive (uncaring)
Unfeeling (callous)

67 **Aquarius Adjective** Theme Words Listed Alphabetically

Allocates (dispenses)
Aloof (reserved)
Alternates (rotates)
Altruistic (humanitarian)
Apathetic (callous)
Apportions (divides)
Approachable (friendly)
Assembles (gathers together)
Associates with (befriends)
Assorted (diversified)
Befriends (affiliates with)
Blends (combines)
Callous (insensitive)
Calls (summons)
Circulates (scatters)
Civic (municipal)

Clinical (impersonal)
Combines (blends)
Communal (common)
Contemporary (modern)
Crammed (congested)
Crowded (packed)
Detached (cool or distant)
Different (unique)
Dispenses (disburses)
Disperses (distributes)
Diversified (varied)
Divides (apportions)
Fraternizes (mingles) with
Friendly (companionable)
Full (filled)
Governmental (legislative)

Humanitarian (altruistic)
Impersonal (uninvolved)
Independent (separate from)
Individualistic (independent)
Insensitive (uncaring)
Integrated (nonsectarian)
Invites (summons)
Lawmaking (political)
Legislative (lawmaking)
Mixes (combines)
Modern (contemporary)
Municipal (civic)
Neighborly (friendly)
Novel (new)
Objective (impartial)
Open (accessible)
Original (independent)
Parliamentary (legislative)

Political (civil)
Progressive (trend-setting)
Removed (aloof)
Reserved (indifferent)
Rotates (switches)
Scatters (strews)
Scrambles (mixes)
Shifts (switches)
Stands Apart (separate from)
Strews (throws around)
Summons (invites)
Switches (varies)
Teeming (filled)
Tolerant (humanitarian)
Unconcerned (uninterested)
Unfeeling (callous)
Unique (distinct)

Aquarius (Noun)

Aquarius (Noun) Essence

Aquarius nouns bring an interest in the gathering and summoning of friends, those who share like-minded interests. Perhaps bringing on inter-action within a group that shares common goals. The idea of membership, of belonging, of participating in events and agendas that are arranged to include many topics of mutual interest remains strong. Such can become the Aquarius noun social focus for being, even their point of concentration. A need to remain detached, perhaps a front of disinterest, can be shown here.

Community or social groups become a meeting place for friends, a place to fraternize or socialize within the assembly. Friends are gathered for social purposes, social growth, and involvement for all remains important. Interest in political and civic interests remains. Often there is a crowding and tightness to the spaces where such activities take place. Allocation of resources, and the sharing of what is available for distribution require constant attention and updates. When these energies are not appeased though there can be an abrupt cutting off of contact that can set others off. Participate, share, hold a common interest, or be left out of consideration.

Aquarius nouns can include an authoritarian thrust, that is, participate in the way intended or be shut out from activities. There is a need to push for the new, for pursuing ideas and interests that lie excluded and outside of the common mainstream's acceptance. Aquarius nouns do not want to maintain the status-quo, there are new ideas and directions to be followed. When so followed then progress moves on. There is an altruistic sense that prevails here, a sense that all are equal within the same body of ideas, as long as they conform to those and do not set themselves aside.

Aquarius nouns show a need to exercise some restraint though lest the number of supporters, those who have been invited, and those who have joined due to mutual interests, become so large that the spaces available for participation become crowded. Groupings can produce a feeling of tightness, of restriction, and when that happens then disinterest in maintaining the same directions forward may bring on an indifference for those prior aims.

19 **Aquarius Noun** Themes Grouped
Compiled from a Base of about 637 Words

Friendship (fellowship)
Brotherhood (camaraderie)
Fraternizing (socialization)
Socialization (mingling)

Crowd (throng)
Throng (crowd)
Coalition (gathering)
Gathering (assemblage)

Community (society)
Society (community)
Company (group)
Membership (company)

Summoning (bringing together)
Invitation (summoning)
Networking (seeking cooperation)
Convention (assembly)

Forward-Looking (trendsetter)
Trendsetting (modernization)
Modernization (updating)
Avant-garde (trendsetter)

Supporter (backer)
Advocate (endorser)
Backer (supporter)
Endorser (backer)

Friend (companion)
Companion (friend)
Crony (friend)
Associate (companion)

Coexistence (existing together)
Outreach (altruism)
Altruism (humanitarianism)
Teamwork (pulling together)

Allocation (distribution)
Sharing (participation)
Dispersal (allotting)
Distribution (dispersion)

Crowding (packing in)
Tightness (packed in)
Congestion (crowding)
Closeness (crowding)

Grouping (bunching)
Amassing (collecting)
Assortment (arrangement)
Allocation (sorting)

Commingling (blend)
Integration (commingling)
Mixture (blend)
Blending (combining)

Diversity (mixture)
Variation (diversity)
Difference (variation)
Departure (diversity)

Detachment (disinterest)
Disinterest (indifference)
Indifference (unconcern)
Impartiality (dispassion)

Insensitivity (callousness)
Authoritarianism (coldness)
Coldness (aloofness)
Unconcern (indifference)

Eccentricity (peculiarity)
Autonomy (freedom)

Nonconformist (individualist)
Uniqueness (distinguishment)

Alienation (rebellion)
Insubordination (disobedience)
Rebellion (insurrection)
Irreverence (indifference)

Impudence (effrontery)
Effrontery (impudence)
Brashness (arrogance)
Audacity (nerve)

New Age Ideas (open to the novel)
Occult Science (astrology)
Receptivity to the New

75 **Aquarius Noun** Theme Words Listed Alphabetically

Advocate (endorser)
Alienation (rebellion)
Allocation (distribution)
Allocation (sorting)
Altruism (humanitarianism)
Amassing (collecting)
Associate (companion)
Assortment (arrangement)
Audacity (nerve)
Authoritarianism (coldness)
Autonomy (freedom)
Avant-garde (trendsetter)
Backer (supporter)
Blending (combining)
Brashness (arrogance)
Brotherhood (camaraderie)
Closeness (crowding)
Coalition (gathering)
Coexistence (existing together)
Coldness (aloofness)
Commingling (blend)
Community (society)
Companion (friend)
Company (group)
Congestion (crowding)
Convention (assembly)
Crony (friend)
Crowd (throng)

Crowding (packing in)
Departure (diversity)
Detachment (disinterest)
Difference (variation)
Disinterest (indifference)
Dispersal (allotting)
Distribution (dispersion)
Diversity (mixture)
Eccentricity (peculiarity)
Effrontery (impudence)
Endorser (backer)
Forward-Looking (trendsetter)
Fraternizing (socialization)
Friend (companion)
Friendship (fellowship)
Gathering (assemblage)
Grouping (bunching)
Impartiality (dispassion)
Impudence (effrontery)
Indifference (unconcern)
Insensitivity (callousness)
Insubordination (disobedience)
Integration (commingling)
Invitation (summoning)
Irreverence (indifference)
Membership (company)
Mixture (blend)
Modernization (updating)

Networking (seeking cooperation)
New Age Ideas (open to the novel)
Nonconformist (individualist)
Occult Science (astrology)
Outreach (altruism)
Rebellion (insurrection)
Receptivity to the New
Sharing (participation)
Socialization (mingling)
Society (community)

Summoning (bringing together)
Supporter (backer)
Teamwork (pulling together)
Throng (crowd)
Tightness (packed in)
Trendsetting (modernization)
Unconcern (indifference)
Uniqueness (distinguishment)
Variation (diversity)

For Notations

Pisces

Rulers: Yang Jupiter and Yin Neptune

Pisces (Adjective) Essence

Pisces adjectives highlight a focus on showing concern and sympathy for others and their interests. They seek to empathize devotion and loyalty to be obliging and appeasing. They can show a compliant and submissive side, and yet may also be somewhat timid and shy. There may also be vagueness to their intentions, and they usually tend to avoid confrontation. Perhaps a feeling of having to take the blame, or remain passive, comes into play. One central idea for them is to have freedom of movement, the ability to let go and to take a new path or direction in life when and as needed.

The concept of forgiveness, of showing mercy and being lenient remains strong here. Pisces adjectives bring a submissive and compliant side, but there are no pushovers here. Pisces adjectives present and display a sensitive and compassionate side, as their intention is to show that their care and concerns are also included in their need to be accommodating and placating. Pisces adjectives may take this as a healing effort on their part to ease the concerns and care of others when such, in their opinion, is needed.

An inner strength within the Pisces adjective themes is their ability to show mercy, to know when to forgive and to move on past prior hurts and/or troubles. This may involve practicing healing or doing some charitable service just to show that their present care and concern for events and people is more than a sympathy or pity for their condition. They are usually able to adapt well to conditions, and may in fact go along with events far more than many others without this basic Pisces adjective influence.

Pisces adjectives show a susceptibility, a trusting, and can be taken in by others because they assume good intentions in what is being presented. This deception usually happens when they are overwhelmed with a variety of impressions or feelings. By opening their inner selves up to others in a trusting way they can succumb to the impassioned efforts of others to enlist their sympathies. Yet their need for freedom, release, stays strong.

21 **Pisces Adjective** Themes Grouped
Compiled from a Base of about 851 Words

Sympathetic (compassionate)
Concerned (regardful)
Sensitive (susceptible)
Pitying (sympathizing)

Alleviating (mitigating)
Mitigating (alleviating)
Relieving (soothing)
Healing (relieving)

Devoted (faithful)
Faithful (loyal)
Loyal (faithful)
Reliable (loyal)

Placating (appeasing)
Accommodating (appeasing)
Obliging (agreeable)
Appeasing (placating)

Compliant (yielding)
Submissive (yielding)
Adapts (adjusts) to
Yielding (compliant)

Merciful (forgiving)
Lenient (merciful)
Soft-Hearted (merciful)
Charitable (merciful)

Freeing (liberating)
Absolving (releasing)
Pardoning (forgiving)
Releasing (freeing)

Shy (bashful)
Timid (bashful)
Bashful (shy)
Reclusive (withdrawn)

Susceptible (trusting)
Trusting (susceptible)
Oversensitive (impressionable)
Gullible (easily fooled)

Vague (ambiguous)
Evasive (vague)
Ambiguous (equivocal)
Digressive (vague)

Avoids (ignores)
Disregards (ignores)
Ignores (disregards)
Rejects (spurns)

Alone (separate)
Solitary (by oneself)
Forgotten (overlooked)
Lonely (friendless)

Abandoned (shunned)
Shunned (disregarded)
Isolated (secluded)
Unclaimed (abandoned)

Wandering (roaming)
Drifting (wandering)
Baseless (drifting)
Escaped (on the loose)

Abandons (deserts)
Gone (missing)
Forsakes (abandons)
Deserts (runs out on)

Hopeless (pointless)
Futile (hopeless)
Aimless (hopeless)
Immaterial (irrelevant)

Confined (constrained)
Disabled (incapacitated)
Restricted (confined)

Shut-In (confined)

Guilty (liable)
Blamable (at fault)
At Fault (guilty)
Inexcusable (unjustifiable)

Passive (yielding)
Tolerant (passive)
Cowardly (gutless)
Fearful (afraid)

Disguised (masked)
Shrouded (cloaked)
Camouflaged (disguised)
Incognito (unidentified)

Groveling (begging)
Begging (beseeching)
Funded (endowed)
Soliciting (begging)

84 **Pisces Adjective** Theme Words Listed Alphabetically

Abandoned (shunned)
Abandons (deserts)
Absolving (releasing)
Accommodating (appeasing)
Adapts (adjusts) to
Aimless (hopeless)
Alleviating (mitigating)
Alone (separate)
Ambiguous (equivocal)
Appeasing (placating)
At Fault (guilty)
Avoids (ignores)
Baseless (drifting)
Bashful (shy)
Begging (beseeching)
Blamable (at fault)
Camouflaged (disguised)
Charitable (merciful)
Compliant (yielding)
Concerned (regardful)
Confined (constrained)
Cowardly (gutless)
Deserts (runs out on)
Devoted (faithful)
Digressive (vague)
Disabled (incapacitated)
Disguised (masked)
Disregards (ignores)
Drifting (wandering)

Escaped (on the loose)
Evasive (vague)
Faithful (loyal)
Fearful (afraid)
Forgotten (overlooked)
Forsakes (abandons)
Freeing (liberating)
Funded (endowed)
Futile (hopeless)
Gone (missing)
Groveling (begging)
Guilty (liable)
Gullible (easily fooled)
Healing (relieving)
Hopeless (pointless)
Ignores (disregards)
Immaterial (irrelevant)
Incognito (unidentified)
Inexcusable (unjustifiable)
Isolated (secluded)
Lenient (merciful)
Lonely (friendless)
Loyal (faithful)
Merciful (forgiving)
Mitigating (alleviating)
Obliging (agreeable)
Oversensitive (impressionable)
Pardoning (forgiving)
Passive (yielding)

Pitying (sympathizing)
Placating (appeasing)
Reclusive (withdrawn)
Rejects (spurns)
Releasing (freeing)
Reliable (loyal)
Relieving (soothing)
Restricted (confined)
Sensitive (susceptible)
Shrouded (cloaked)
Shunned (disregarded)
Shut-In (confined)
Shy (bashful)

Soft-Hearted (merciful)
Soliciting (begging)
Solitary (by oneself)
Submissive (yielding)
Susceptible (trusting)
Sympathetic (compassionate)
Timid (bashful)
Tolerant (passive)
Trusting (susceptible)
Unclaimed (abandoned)
Vague (ambiguous)
Wandering (roaming)
Yielding (compliant)

Pisces (Noun)

Pisces (Noun) Essence

Pisces nouns focus on exoneration, the clearing and forgiving of those injustices or wrongdoings that linger and occupy time and energy. The need for releasing, letting go, and finding a way to move out of past encumbrances remains strong. Once the realization that the need to carry emotional burdens from past interactions is not needed then the power of release, forgiveness and liberation can be brought into play. One way to do this is to show clemency, a way to release and let go of past burdens. Showing toleration in times of stress can be a helpful way of doing this.

Devotion and fidelity remain as important parts of the Pisces noun themes. Learning the inner meaning and application of being faithful, even though this may cause some emotional pain, becomes important. If it becomes necessary to yield, to submit to forces or circumstances that may not be what one desires, then the energies here can help with assisting and bringing a closure to events or actions past. Learning to look beyond the obvious actions of the present, and to see the underlying issues that form reality becomes a good use of the Pisces noun motif.

Giving amnesty and seeking forgiveness can produce feelings of release and liberation. There is a call here for leniency and alleviation of burdens being imposed. Pisces nouns show a need to accept sacrifice and penance while dealing out compassion and solace. There is a preference here to have an avenue of escape, to ignore or overlook situations that can be avoided. A preference remains to be alone, or for being shy, even reclusive.

An important Pisces nouns theme idea is exoneration, the clearing and forgiving of those injustices or wrongdoings that linger and occupy time and energy. The need for releasing, letting go, and finding a way to move out of past encumbrances remains strong. Once the realization that the need to carry emotional burdens from past interactions is not needed then the power of release, forgiveness and liberation can be brought into play. One way to do this is to show clemency, a way to release and a letting go of past burdens. Showing toleration in times of stress can also be a helpful way of doing this.

18 **Pisces Noun** Themes Grouped
Compiled from a Base of about 833 Words

Exoneration (clearing)
Acquittal (exoneration)
Amnesty (forgiveness)
Forgiveness (pardoning)

Exemption (release)
Release (letting go)
Freedom (release)
Liberation (freeing)

Leniency (mercy)
Clemency (leniency)
Mercy (leniency)
Tolerance (lenience)

Alleviation (respite)
Mitigation (alleviation)
Respite (letup)
Relief (comfort)

Penance (atonement)
Atonement (penance)
Reparation (redress or amends)
Sacrifice (yielding)

Sympathy (compassion)
Solace (consolation)
Concern (attention)
Compassion (sympathy)

Devotion (dedication)
Loyalty (faithfulness)
Dedication (devotion)
Fidelity (loyalty)

Submission (yielding)
Acquiescence (submission)
Appeasement (submission)
Capitulation (submission)

Desertion (relinquishing)
Forsaking (deserted)
Renunciation (abdication)
Sacrifice (self-denial)

Escape (avoidance)
Seclusion (isolation)
Disguise (false front)
Withdrawal (secession)

Avoiding (ignoring)
Ignoring (overlooking)
Overlooking (avoiding)
Shirking (evading)

Alone (lonely)
Forgotten (abandoned)
Lonesome (unwanted)
Deserted (abandoned)

Confinement (restriction)
Restriction (confinement)
Incapacity (disability)
Constrained (restricted)

Insecurity (self-doubt)
Self-Doubt (insecurity)
Failing (shortcoming)
Helplessness (powerlessness)

Susceptibility (sensitiveness)
Suggestibility (receptiveness)
Sensitivity (impressionability)
Gullibility (innocence)

Shortcoming (drawback)
Fault (blameability)
Blame (guilt or fault)
Guilt (self-accusation)

Bashfulness (reclusiveness)
Reclusiveness (withdrawal)
Hesitation (timidity)
Solitude (seclusion)

Solicitation (asking)
Welfare (allotment)
Compensation (welfare)

71 **Pisces Noun Theme** Words Listed Alphabetically

Acquiescence (submission)
Acquittal (exoneration)
Alleviation (respite)
Alone (lonely)
Amnesty (forgiveness)
Appeasement (submission)
Atonement (penance)
Avoiding (ignoring)
Bashfulness (reclusiveness)
Blame (guilt or fault)
Capitulation (submission)
Clemency (leniency)
Compassion (sympathy)
Compensation (welfare)

Concern (attention)
Confinement (restriction)
Constrained (restricted)
Dedication (devotion)
Deserted (abandoned)
Desertion (relinquishing)
Devotion (dedication)
Disguise (false front)
Escape (avoidance)
Exemption (release)
Exoneration (clearing)
Failing (shortcoming)
Fault (blameability)
Fidelity (loyalty)

Forgiveness (pardoning)
Forgotten (abandoned)
Forsaking (deserted)
Freedom (release)
Guilt (self-accusation)
Gullibility (innocence)
Helplessness (powerlessness)
Hesitation (timidity)
Ignoring (overlooking)
Incapacity (disability)
Insecurity (self-doubt)
Leniency (mercy)
Liberation (freeing)
Lonesome (unwanted)
Loyalty (faithfulness)
Mercy (leniency)
Mitigation (alleviation)
Overlooking (avoiding)
Penance (atonement)
Reclusiveness (withdrawal)
Release (letting go)
Relief (comfort)

Renunciation (abdication)
Reparation (redress or amends)
Respite (let up)
Restriction (confinement)
Sacrifice (self-denial)
Sacrifice (yielding)
Seclusion (isolation)
Self-Doubt (insecurity)
Sensitivity (impressionability)
Shirking (evading)
Shortcoming (drawback)
Solace (consolation)
Solicitation (asking)
Solitude (seclusion)
Submission (yielding)
Suggestibility (receptiveness)
Susceptibility (sensitiveness)
Sympathy (compassion)
Tolerance (lenience)
Welfare (allotment)
Withdrawl (secession)

For Notations

An Alphabetical list of all Sign Keyword Themes

1731 Entries

Abandoned (shunned)	psc	A	Accreditation (standards)	cap	N
Abandons (deserts)	psc	A	Accumulation (bringing in)	can	N
Ability (competence)	cap	N	Accuracy (precision)	vir	N
Absentmindedness (inattention)	sag	N	Accurate (factual)	vir	A
			Accusation (complaint)	lib	N
Absolving (releasing)	psc	A	Accuses (implicates)	lib	A
Absorbed (obsessed)	sco	A	Acknowledgment (assent)	lib	N
Absorbs (soaks in)	can	A	Acquiescence (submission)	psc	N
Absorption (consummation)	can	N	Acquittal (exoneration)	psc	N
Academic (schooled)	gem	A	Action (movement)	ari	N
Acclaim (approval)	leo	N	Actuality (certainty)	cap	N
Accommodating (appeasing)	psc	A	Adaptability (flexibility)	gem	N
Accommodation (compromise)	lib	N	Adapts (adjusts) to	psc	A
			Addresses (greets)	ari	A
Accommodation (shelter)	can	N	Adhesive (glue)	can	A
Accountability (responsibility)	cap	N	Adjacent (adjoining)	gem	A
Accountable (beholden)	lib	A	Adjustment (compromise)	lib	N
Accountable (responsible)	cap	A	Adjustment (repair)	vir	N

Adjusts for (suits)	lib	A	Allegiance (commitment)	sco	N
Administration (supervision)	cap	N	Allegorical (legendary)	sag	A
Administrative (organized)	cap	A	Allegory (myth)	sag	N
Admonishment (scolding)	sco	N	Alleviating (mitigating)	psc	A
Adulation (praise)	leo	N	Alleviation (respite)	psc	N
Advancement (motion forward)	ari	N	Allocates (dispenses)	aqu	A
			Allocation (distribution)	aqu	N
Advancing (proceeding)	ari	A	Allocation (sorting)	aqu	N
Adventure (exploration)	sag	N	Alone (lonely)	psc	N
Adventurous (footloose)	sag	A	Alone (separate)	psc	A
Advocate (endorser)	aqu	N	Aloof (reserved)	aqu	A
Affection (emotion)	leo	N	Alternates (rotates)	aqu	A
Affection (feeling)	can	N	Alternative (another)	lib	N
Affectionate (loving)	leo	A	Altruism (humanitarianism)	aqu	N
Agility (nimbleness)	gem	N	Altruistic (humanitarian)	aqu	A
Agreeing (concurring)	lib	A	Amasses (collects)	can	A
Agreement (acknowledgment)	lib	N	Amassing (collecting)	aqu	N
Agriculture (farming)	can	N	Ambiguity (vagueness)	sag	N
Aiding (assisting)	vir	A	Ambiguous (equivocal)	psc	A
Aim (intention)	cap	N	Ambition (initiative)	cap	N
Aimless (hopeless)	psc	A	Ambitious (enterprising)	cap	A
Alertness (watchfulness)	can	N	Ambivalent (undecided)	lib	A
Alienated (opposed)	lib	A	Amends (compensation)	sco	N
Alienation (rebellion)	aqu	N	Amidst (between)	lib	A
Aligned (neat)	vir	A	Amnesty (forgiveness)	psc	N
Alike (agreeing)	lib	A	Amusing (entertaining)	leo	A
Alike (similar)	gem	A	Analogy (comparison)	sag	N
All-Inclusive (sweeping)	sag	A	Analysis (study)	sco	N

Analyzes (examines)	sco	A	Arid (dry)	ari	A
Ancestry (lineage)	can	N	Arising (ascending)	cap	N
Announcement (communication)	gem	N	Aristocratic (dignified)	leo	A
			Arousing (inciting)	ari	A
Anthropomorphic (human shaped)	sag	A	Arrangement (organization)	vir	N
			Arrival (appearance)	ari	N
Anthropomorphism	sag	N	Arriving (proceeding)	ari	A
Anticipation (expectation)	ari	N	Arrogance (pride)	leo	N
Anxiety (worry)	vir	N	Arrogant (smug)	leo	A
Apathetic (callous)	aqu	A	Articulate (talkative)	gem	A
Apparatus (equipment)	vir	N	Ascent (moving upwards)	cap	N
Appeasement (submission)	psc	N	Ashen (pale)	lib	A
Appeasing (placating)	psc	A	Asking (inquisitive)	gem	A
Applicability (properness)	cap	N	Aspiration (ambition)	cap	N
Applicability (relevance)	lib	N	Assembles (gathers together)	aqu	A
Appoints (designates)	ari	A	Assent (agreement)	lib	N
Apportions (divides)	aqu	A	Assertive (confronting)	ari	A
Approach (coming nearer)	ari	N	Assistance (helping)	vir	N
Approachable (friendly)	aqu	A	Associate (companion)	aqu	N
Approaching (preliminary)	ari	A	Associates with (befriends)	aqu	A
Appropriate (befitting)	cap	A	Assorted (diversified)	aqu	A
Appropriate (suitable)	lib	A	Assortment (arrangement)	aqu	N
Approved (official)	cap	A	Assumed (concocted)	sag	A
Approximate (estimated)	sag	A	Assumed (pretended)	leo	A
Aptness (usefulness)	cap	N	Assumption (guess)	sag	N
Ardent (arousing)	ari	A	Assurance (commitment)	sco	N
Ardor (affection)	leo	N	Astray (off-the-mark)	sag	A
Arduous (demanding)	cap	A	At Fault (guilty)	psc	A

At fault (liable)	lib	A	Bashfulness (reclusiveness)	psc	N
At Issue (opposed)	lib	A	Beard (whiskers)	can	N
Atonement (penance)	psc	N	Befitting (suitable)	lib	A
Attaches (secures)	can	A	Befriends (affiliates with)	aqu	A
Attachment (reliance)	can	N	Begging (beseeching)	psc	A
Attainable (reachable)	cap	A	Beginning (introduction)	ari	N
Attempt (undertaking)	ari	N	Beginning (starting)	ari	A
Attentive (faithful)	vir	A	Beloved (cherished)	can	A
Attire (clothing)	vir	N	Bendable (adjustable)	gem	A
Attired (dressed)	vir	A	Betrayal (breach of faith)	sco	N
Attuned (harmonized)	lib	A	Betrothal (proposal of marriage)	lib	N
Audacity (forwardness)	ari	N			
Audacity (nerve)	aqu	N	Between (amidst)	lib	A
Authoritarianism (coldness)	aqu	N	Binding (obligated)	sco	A
Authoritative (official)	cap	A	Blamable (at fault)	psc	A
Authorization (permission)	sco	N	Blame (guilt or fault)	psc	N
Autonomy (freedom)	aqu	N	Blameless (guiltless)	tau	A
Avant-garde (trendsetter)	aqu	N	Blatant (conspicuous)	leo	A
Avoiding (ignoring)	psc	N	Blending (combining)	aqu	N
Avoids (ignores)	psc	A	Blends (combines)	aqu	A
Awkward (clumsy)	tau	A	Blessed (sainted)	vir	A
Backer (supporter)	aqu	N	Bluff (open deception)	sag	N
Baffling (puzzling)	sco	N	Blunt (dull)	tau	A
Balance (equilibrium)	lib	N	Boastful (bragging)	leo	A
Balanced (equalized)	lib	A	Boasting (bragging)	leo	N
Barricade (deterrent)	can	N	Boldness (daring)	ari	N
Baseless (drifting)	psc	A	Boldness (initiative)	cap	N
Bashful (shy)	psc	A	Bossy (domineering)	sco	A

Brashness (arrogance)	aqu	N	Careful (cautious)	cap	A
Break-Up (separation)	lib	N	Casual (informal)	sag	A
Bridal (nuptial)	lib	A	Category (grouping)	vir	N
Bright (literate)	gem	A	Cautious (prudent)	cap	A
Bringing In (collecting)	can	N	Cavity (pit or hole)	can	N
Broad Picture (overview)	sag	N	Celibacy (self-restraint)	vir	N
Broad-Minded (idealistic)	sag	A	Celibate (chaste)	vir	A
Brooding (moping)	can	N	Ceremonial (formal)	vir	A
Brotherhood (camaraderie)	aqu	N	Ceremony (ritual)	vir	N
Brusque (abrupt)	ari	A	Certain (sure)	ari	A
Bulge (lump)	leo	N	Certainty (validity)	cap	N
Bulk (mass or substance)	tau	N	Certification (accreditation)	cap	N
Bulky (massive)	tau	A	Certified (authentic)	vir	A
Bungling (awkwardness)	tau	N	Challenge (purpose)	ari	N
Businesslike (practical)	cap	A	Challenge (rivalry)	lib	N
Busy (occupied)	cap	A	Challenging (assertive)	ari	A
Bygone (past)	can	A	Characteristic (feature)	vir	N
Callous (insensitive)	aqu	A	Charitable (merciful)	psc	A
Calls (summons)	aqu	A	Chase the	sag	N
Calm (collected)	tau	A	(pursuit as in a game)		
Calmness (composure)	tau	N	Chaste (virginal)	vir	A
Camouflaged (disguised)	psc	A	Cheap (economical)	cap	A
Candid (direct)	sag	A	Cheer (high spirits)	leo	N
Candidness (directness)	sag	N	Cheerful (gleeful)	leo	A
Capable (qualified)	cap	A	Cherished (esteemed)	can	A
Capitulation (submission)	psc	N	Cherishing (holding dear)	can	N
Care (accuracy)	vir	N	Chic (fashionable)	leo	A
Carefree (unconcerned)	tau	A	Chides (scolds)	sco	A

Childbirth (beginnings)	leo	N	Closing (securing)	can	N
Choice (alternative)	lib	N	Clothed (dressed)	vir	A
Choosy (particular)	vir	N	Clothing (attire or outfit)	vir	N
Chubby (plump)	tau	A	Clumsiness (being ungraceful)	tau	N
Churchy (religious)	sag	A	Clumsy (lacking grace)	tau	A
Circulates (scatters)	aqu	A	Clutches (grasps)	can	A
Civic (municipal)	aqu	A	Coalition (gathering)	aqu	N
Civil (polite)	lib	A	Coequal (equivalent)	lib	A
Claimed (alleged)	leo	A	Coercion (pressure)	ari	N
Clarification (excuse)	sag	N	Coexistence (existing together)	aqu	N
Clarification (explanation)	gem	N	Cogitation (thinking)	gem	N
Clarity (unambiguity)	lib	N	Coldness (aloofness)	aqu	N
Classical (traditional)	can	A	Collects (accumulates)	can	A
Classifies (organizes)	vir	A	Coloration (fabrication)	leo	N
Clean (hygienic)	vir	A	Combines (blends)	aqu	A
Clean (unmarked)	lib	A	Comfortable (relaxed)	tau	A
Cleanliness (neatness)	vir	N	Commingling (blend)	aqu	N
Cleanliness (purity)	lib	N	Commitment (pledge)	sco	N
Clear (explicit)	vir	A	Committed (obligated)	sco	A
Clear (transparent)	lib	A	Communal (common)	aqu	A
Clemency (leniency)	psc	N	Communication (exchange of information)	gem	N
Cleverness (ingenuity)	gem	N			
Climbing (ascending)	cap	N	Community (society)	aqu	N
Clings to (holds)	can	A	Compacted (dense)	sco	A
Clinical (impersonal)	aqu	A	Companion (friend)	aqu	N
Close (nearest)	can	A	Company (group)	aqu	N
Closeness (crowding)	aqu	N	Comparison (analogy)	sag	N
Closes (secures)	can	A	Comparison (correlation)	lib	N

Compassion (sympathy)	psc	N	Concoction (fabrication)	sag	N
Compatible (fits with)	lib	A	Concurrent (simultaneous)	lib	A
Compelled (pressed)	sco	A	Concurring (agreeing)	lib	A
Compensating (equalized)	lib	A	Conditional (hinging on)	can	A
Compensation (welfare)	psc	N	Confidentiality (privacy)	sco	N
Competence (performance)	cap	N	Confined (constrained)	psc	A
Competition (rivalry)	lib	N	Confinement (restriction)	psc	N
Complacent (untroubled)	tau	A	Confirms (establishes)	sco	A
Complaining (critical)	vir	A	Conflict (clash of ideas)	lib	N
Complaint (accusation)	lib	N	Conformity (consistency)	lib	N
Complaint (criticism)	vir	N	Conformity (obedience)	vir	N
Complementary (paired)	lib	A	Conformity (sameness)	tau	N
Compliance (obedience)	vir	N	Confrontation (clash)	lib	N
Compliant (yielding)	psc	A	Confronting (tackling)	ari	A
Component (fragment)	vir	N	Congestion (crowding)	aqu	N
Component (part of)	vir	A	Conjectural (theoretical)	sag	A
Component (source)	can	N	Conjecture (speculation)	sag	N
Comprehensive (inclusive)	sag	A	Consent (privilege)	sco	N
Compromise (accommodation)	lib	N	Conservative (opposed to change)	tau	A
Compulsory (forced)	sco	A	Considers (deliberates over)	lib	A
Conceit (egomania)	ari	N	Consistency (regularity)	tau	N
Conceit (pride)	leo	N	Consistency (uniformity)	lib	N
Concentrated (dense)	sco	A	Consistent (regular)	cap	A
Concept (idea)	sag	N	Conspicuous (prominent)	leo	A
Concern (attention)	psc	N	Constrained (restricted)	psc	N
Concerned (regardful)	psc	A	Constructive (helpful)	vir	A
Concocted (cooked up)	sag	A	Consumable (ingestible)	can	A

Consumption (use of goods)	can	N	(opposite number)		
Contagious (infectious)	vir	A	Counting (enumeration)	vir	N
Contemplative (cerebral)	gem	A	Countrified (rural)	can	A
Contemporary (modern)	aqu	A	Courage (daring)	ari	N
Contentment (satisfaction)	tau	N	Covering (exterior)	can	N
Contents (components)	can	N	Cowardice (timidity)	leo	N
Contradiction	lib	N	Cowardly (gutless)	psc	A
(opposing statement)			Crabbiness (grouchiness)	can	N
Contrast (difference)	lib	N	Craftiness (know-how)	gem	N
Contrasted to (opposite)	lib	A	Crammed (congested)	aqu	A
Control (enforcement)	sco	N	Cranky (moody)	can	A
Controls (manipulates)	sco	A	Creation (beginning)	ari	N
Controversial (debatable)	lib	A	Crested (ridged)	leo	A
Convenience (handiness)	gem	N	Critical (fussy)	vir	A
Convention (assembly)	aqu	N	Criticism (gripe)	vir	N
Conventional (regular)	tau	A	Critique (criticism)	vir	N
Conversation (talk)	gem	N	Crony (friend)	aqu	N
Convinced (opinionated)	ari	A	Crop Raising (farming)	can	N
Cooked (prepared)	vir	A	Crossing Over (clearing)	sag	N
Cooking (preparing food)	can	N	Crowd (throng)	aqu	N
Cooperation (teamwork)	lib	N	Crowded (packed)	aqu	A
Cooperative (mutual)	lib	A	Crowding (packing in)	aqu	N
Correct (genuine)	vir	A	Crumbly (flaky)	can	A
Correction (adjustment)	vir	N	Cryptic (inscrutable)	sco	N
Correlation (analogy)	sag	N	Culture (intellectual taste)	lib	N
Correlation (comparison)	lib	N	Cunning (devious)	sco	A
Corrupt (depraved)	sco	A	Curable (treatable)	vir	A
Counterpart	lib	N	Cures (remedial treatments)	vir	N

Curiosity (questioning)	gem	N	Deserted (abandoned)	psc	N
Curious (inquisitive)	gem	A	Desertion (relinquishing)	psc	N
Curt (impolite)	ari	A	Deserts (runs out on)	psc	A
Custom (convention)	can	N	Designates (names)	ari	A
Dandyish (showy)	leo	A	Detached (cool or distant)	aqu	A
Dapper (neat)	leo	A	Detachment (disinterest)	aqu	N
Daring (fearlessness)	ari	N	Detail (feature)	vir	N
Dashing (showy)	leo	A	Determinable (verifiable)	gem	A
Debatable (questionable)	lib	A	Determination (findings)	sco	N
Decent (proper)	lib	A	Determination (resolve)	cap	N
Decides (determines)	lib	A	Determined (positive)	ari	A
Dedication (devotion)	psc	N	Determined (willful)	sco	A
Defense (protection)	can	N	Developing (growing)	tau	A
Defensive (protective)	can	A	Devious (sneaky)	sco	A
Deliberate (intended)	sco	A	Devised (contrived)	sag	A
Demanding (stern)	cap	A	Devoted (attentive)	vir	A
Denies (rejects)	sco	A	Devoted (faithful)	psc	A
Dense (compact)	sco	A	Devotion (dedication)	psc	N
Density (substance or solidity)	tau	N	Dialog (conversation)	gem	N
Departure (diversity)	aqu	N	Dictatorial (domineering)	sco	A
Dependable (prompt)	cap	A	Diet (nutritional regimen)	vir	N
Dependable (reliable)	tau	A	Difference (variation)	aqu	N
Dependence (reliance on)	can	N	Different (unique)	aqu	A
Dependent on (relying on)	can	A	Digestible (edible)	can	A
Depletion (using up)	can	N	Digestion (absorbing food)	vir	N
Descendants (offspring)	can	N	Digestive (assimilative)	vir	A
Describes (explains)	gem	A	Digestive Issues (distresses)	vir	N
Description (portrayal)	gem	N	Digestive Processes	can	N

Dignified (distinguished)	leo	A	Dissimilar (incompatible)	lib	A
Dignity (stateliness)	leo	N	Distant (remote)	sag	A
Digression (long-windedness)	sag	N	Distinct (clear)	vir	A
Digressive (rambling)	sag	A	Distinct (explicit)	gem	A
Digressive (vague)	psc	A	Distinction (renown)	leo	N
Diligent (persistent)	cap	A	Distress (illness)	vir	N
Direct (forthright)	sag	A	Distribution (dispersion)	aqu	N
Directives (orders)	cap	N	Diversified (varied)	aqu	A
Dirty (begrimed)	ari	A	Diversion (recreation)	leo	N
Disabled (incapacitated)	psc	A	Diversity (mixture)	aqu	N
Disagreeable (irritable)	can	A	Divided (shared)	lib	A
Disagreeing (at variance)	lib	A	Divides (apportions)	aqu	A
Disagreement (dispute)	lib	N	Divorce (separation)	lib	N
Disciplines (chastises)	sco	A	Dogmatic (opinionated)	ari	A
Discriminates (distinguishes)	vir	A	Domestic (home loving)	can	A
Discussing (mentioning)	gem	A	Domineering (intimidating)	sco	A
Discussion (talking)	gem	N	Double (accommodates two)	gem	A
Disguise (false front)	psc	N	Doubtful (skeptical)	sco	A
Disguised (masked)	psc	A	Downhome (countrified)	can	A
Disinterest (indifference)	aqu	N	Drama (showmanship)	leo	N
Disloyalty (unfaithfulness)	sco	N	Dramatic (theatrical)	leo	A
Dispenses (disburses)	aqu	A	Drenched (saturated)	can	A
Dispersal (allotting)	aqu	N	Dress (attire or clothing)	vir	N
Disperses (distributes)	aqu	A	Dressed (clothed)	vir	A
Display (exhibition)	leo	N	Drifting (wandering)	psc	A
Disputable (debatable)	lib	A	Drill (practice)	vir	N
Dispute (altercation)	lib	N	Drowsiness (sleepiness)	leo	N
Disregards (ignores)	psc	A	Dry (arid)	ari	A

Dryness (aridity)	ari	N	Elaboration (expansion)	sag	N
Duality (replica)	gem	N	Eloquence (fluency)	gem	N
Dull (unsharpened)	tau	A	Eloquent (articulate)	gem	A
Dull-Witted (thickheaded)	tau	A	Elusive (baffling)	sco	A
Duplicated (repeated)	gem	A	Embellished (added to)	sag	A
Duplication (reproduction)	gem	N	Embellishment (pretense)	leo	N
Durability (toughness)	tau	N	Emotion (expression)	leo	N
Dust (fine-grained material)	can	N	Emotional (sentimental)	can	A
Dutiful (conscientious)	vir	A	Emotional Closeness (attachment)	can	N
Duty (service)	vir	N			
Eager (excited)	ari	A	Emotional Responses (outlets)	can	N
Eagerness (urgency)	ari	N	Emphasis (insistence)	ari	N
Early (premature)	ari	A	Emphasized (featured)	ari	A
Earthy (natural)	tau	N	Emphatic (insistent)	ari	A
Easy (effortless)	tau	A	Emptiness (barrenness)	ari	N
Easygoing (calm)	tau	A	Empty (barren)	ari	A
Easygoing (informal)	sag	A	Endorser (backer)	aqu	N
Eccentricity (peculiarity)	aqu	N	Endurance (holding out)	tau	N
Economical (thrifty)	cap	A	Enduring (long-lasting)	tau	A
Edible (eatable)	can	A	Enforcement (crackdown)	sco	N
Educated (learned)	sag	A	Enigma (puzzle)	sco	N
Education (schooling)	gem	N	Enigmatic (puzzling)	sco	A
Educational (instructional)	gem	A	Enrichment (becoming richer)	tau	N
Effective (working)	cap	A	Entertaining (amusing)	leo	A
Effortless (uncomplicated)	tau	A	Entertainment (amusement)	leo	N
Effrontery (impudence)	aqu	N	Entrance (arrival)	ari	N
Egomania (excessive egotism)	ari	N	Environs (surroundings)	can	N
Egotistical (self-important)	leo	A	Equality (parity)	lib	N

Equalized (compensated)	lib	A	Exempted (immune)	sco	A
Equilibrium (equality)	lib	N	Exemption (release)	psc	N
Equipment	vir	N	Exhaustive (painstaking)	cap	A
(apparatus or supplies)			Exoneration (clearing)	psc	N
Equips (furnishes)	vir	A	Exotic (foreign)	sag	A
Equitable (fair)	lib	A	Expecting (approaching)	ari	A
Error in Judgment	sag	N	Expedient (practical)	tau	A
(absentmindedness)			Expedient (useful)	cap	A
Escape (avoidance)	psc	N	Experienced (qualified)	cap	A
Escaped (on the loose)	psc	A	Explains (clarifies)	gem	A
Esoteric (secret)	sco	A	Explanation (account)	gem	N
Estimated (assumed)	sag	A	Explicit (clear)	vir	A
Estimation (guess)	sag	N	Explicit (distinct)	gem	A
Ethical (honest)	cap	A	Exploration (adventure)	sag	N
Evaluation (scrutiny)	vir	N	Exposed (naked)	ari	A
Evasive (vague)	psc	A	Exposed (unobstructed)	sag	A
Exact (factual)	vir	A	Exposed (vulnerable)	can	A
Exacting (painstaking)	vir	A	Expression (emotion)	leo	N
Exaggerated (overstated)	sag	A	Expressive (spontaneous)	leo	A
Exaggeration (overstatement)	sag	N	Extensive (far-flung)	sag	A
Exaltation (praise)	leo	N	Exterior (covering)	can	N
Examination (scrutiny)	vir	N	Exterior (outside)	can	A
Examines (studies)	sco	A	Fabrication (embellishment)	leo	N
Example (sample)	vir	N	Facade (exterior part)	can	N
Exclusion (show of power)	ari	N	Factual (faithful to)	vir	A
Exclusive (preferred)	lib	A	Failing (shortcoming)	psc	N
Excuse (justification)	sag	N	Fair (unbiased)	lib	A
Execution (performance)	cap	N	Fairness (evenhandedness)	lib	N

Faithful (dutiful)	vir	A	Firmness (reliability)	tau	N
Faithful (loyal)	psc	A	Fits with (harmonious)	lib	A
Familiar with (conversant)	gem	A	Fitting (appropriate)	cap	A
Family (family members)	can	N	Fixation (obsession)	sco	N
Famous (eminent)	leo	A	Flag (national emblem)	can	N
Far-Fetched (exaggerated)	sag	A	Flagrant (audacious)	leo	A
Far-Reaching (wide-ranging)	sag	A	Flaking (peeling)	can	A
Farming (growing)	can	N	Flamboyant (showy)	leo	A
Fastening (closing)	can	N	Flattering (laudatory)	leo	A
Fastens (secures)	can	A	Flattery (false compliment)	leo	N
Fastidious (exacting)	vir	A	Flaunted (displayed)	leo	A
Fatty (chubby)	tau	N	Fleshy (fatty)	tau	A
Fault (blameability)	psc	N	Fleshy (substantial)	tau	N
Favored (chosen)	lib	A	Flexibility (suppleness)	gem	N
Fawning (flattering)	leo	A	Flexible (bendable)	gem	A
Fearful (afraid)	psc	A	Flowery (ornate)	leo	A
Feasibility (workability)	tau	N	Fluency (command of language)	gem	N
Feature (characteristic)	vir	N			
Feelings (touch sensations)	tau	N	Focus (preoccupation)	sco	N
Feigned (pretended)	leo	A	Folksy (informal)	sag	A
Festivity (celebration)	leo	N	Following (next)	tau	A
Fibrous (stringy or wiry)	can	A	Foolhardy (reckless)	ari	A
Fidelity (loyalty)	psc	N	Footloose (venturesome)	sag	A
Figuring (computation)	vir	N	Foppish (pompous)	leo	A
Filthiness (dirtiness)	ari	N	Forced (compelled)	sco	A
Finances (funds or capital)	tau	N	Forcing (pushing)	ari	A
Findings (determinations)	sco	N	Foregoes (gives up)	sco	A
Finesse (discretion)	lib	N	Foreign (not native)	sag	A

Foretaste (dirtiness)	ari	N	Frolicsome (playful)	leo	A
Forgiveness (pardoning)	psc	N	Full (filled)	aqu	A
Forgotten (abandoned)	psc	N	Function (purpose)	cap	N
Forgotten (overlooked)	psc	A	Functional (working)	cap	A
Formal (proper)	vir	A	Funded (endowed)	psc	A
Formal (reserved)	cap	A	Fur (hairy covering)	can	N
Formal Union (marriage)	lib	N	Furnishes (provides)	vir	A
Formality (custom)	vir	N	Furry (fuzzy)	can	A
Forsakes (abandons)	psc	A	Furthermost (uttermost)	sag	A
Forsaking (deserted)	psc	N	Fussy (particular)	vir	A
Forthcoming (impending)	tau	A	Futile (hopeless)	psc	A
Fortification (stronghold)	can	N	Fuzz (nap or thatch)	can	N
Forward-Looking (trendsetter)	aqu	N	Garish (gaudy)	leo	A
Founding (establishing)	ari	A	Gathering (assemblage)	aqu	N
Fractional (partial)	vir	A	Gaudiness (garishness)	leo	N
Fragment (portion)	vir	N	Genuine (legal or real)	vir	A
Fragments (fine grains or dust)	can	N	Gesturing (motioning)	gem	A
Frank (open or candid)	sag	A	Glibness (wordiness)	gem	N
Frankness (openness)	sag	N	Glorification (honoring)	leo	N
Fraternizes (mingles) with	aqu	A	Glorified (praised)	leo	A
Fraternizing (socialization)	aqu	N	Gone (missing)	psc	A
Freedom (release)	psc	N	Good-Natured (amiable)	leo	A
Freeing (liberating)	psc	A	Governable (controllable)	cap	A
Fresh (newly made)	ari	A	Governmental (legislative)	aqu	A
Friend (companion)	aqu	N	Grasping (gripping)	can	A
Friendly (companionable)	aqu	A	Grasping (holding on)	can	N
Friendship (fellowship)	aqu	N	Gratification (self-fulfillment)	tau	N
Frolic (gaiety)	leo	N	Greets (welcomes)	ari	A

Gripe (complaint)	vir	N	Health (therapy) Interests	vir	A
Groomed (attired)	vir	A	Helpful (aiding)	vir	A
Grouchy (irritable)	can	A	Helping (assisting)	vir	N
Grounded (stable)	tau	A	Helplessness (powerlessness)	psc	N
Grouping (bunching)	aqu	N	Heretical (unbelieving)	sco	A
Groveling (begging)	psc	A	Hesitation (timidity)	psc	N
Growing (maintaining)	tau	A	Hidden (secretive)	sco	A
Guarded (protected)	can	A	Hinted (rumored)	sag	A
Guess (estimate)	sag	N	Historical (ancient)	can	A
Guidance (instruction)	cap	N	Hit-or-Miss (accidental)	sag	A
Guileless (innocent)	tau	A	Hoarding (stockpiling)	can	N
Guilt (self-accusation)	psc	N	Hoards (collects)	can	A
Guilty (liable)	psc	A	Holding (embracing)	can	A
Gullibility (innocence)	psc	N	Holy (pious)	vir	A
Gullible (easily fooled)	psc	A	Home (residence)	can	N
Gummy (sticky)	can	A	Honest (aboveboard)	cap	A
Hairiness (hirsute)	ari	N	Hopeless (pointless)	psc	A
Hairy (hirsute)	ari	A	Hospitality (sociability)	lib	N
Halved (divided)	lib	A	Household (domestic)	can	A
Handiness (convenience)	gem	N	Housing (lodgings)	can	N
Handy (accessible)	gem	A	Humanitarian (altruistic)	aqu	A
Hardheaded (obstinate)	tau	A	Humility (humbleness)	vir	N
Harmonious (agreeable)	lib	A	Hunch (impression)	sag	N
Harmony (consensus)	lib	N	Hurdling (leaping over)	sag	N
Haste (speed)	ari	N	Hurried (impatient)	ari	A
Hasty (rushed)	ari	A	Hurry (hastiness)	ari	N
Healing (curing)	vir	A	Hygienic (clean)	vir	A
Healing (relieving)	psc	A	Hypothesis (supposition)	sag	N

Idealistic (envisioned)	sag	A	Impulsive (rash)	ari	A
Identifies (labels)	ari	A	Impulsiveness (recklessness)	ari	N
Idleness (lethargy)	leo	N	Inaccurate (imprecise)	sag	A
Ignores (disregards)	psc	A	Inactive (still)	tau	A
Ignoring (overlooking)	psc	N	Inactivity (motionless)	tau	N
Ill (sick)	vir	A	Inadvertent (unintended)	sag	A
Illicit (illegal)	sco	A	Inattention (oversight)	sag	N
Illness (distress)	vir	N	Incapacity (disability)	psc	N
Illustrates (pictures)	gem	A	Incognito (unidentified)	psc	A
Imaginary (hypothetical)	sag	A	Incompatible (unsuited)	lib	A
Imitative (mimicking)	gem	A	Inconsiderate (thoughtless)	ari	A
Immaterial (irrelevant)	psc	A	Inconsistency (discrepancy)	lib	N
Immobility (fixity)	tau	N	Incriminates (implicates)	lib	A
Immune (spared)	sco	A	Indebted (obligated)	sco	A
Impartial (unbiased)	lib	A	Indecision (wavering)	lib	N
Impartiality (dispassion)	aqu	N	Indecisive (wavering)	lib	A
Impatience (rashness)	ari	N	Indefensible (beyond reason)	lib	A
Imperative (command)	ari	N	Indentation (depression)	can	N
Imperious (lordly)	leo	A	Independent (separate from)	aqu	A
Impersonal (uninvolved)	aqu	A	Indication (sign)	ari	N
Impervious (leakproof)	can	A	Indifference (unconcern)	aqu	N
Implicates (incriminates)	lib	A	Indirect (inferred)	sag	A
Impolite (discourteous)	ari	A	Indirect (sidewise)	can	A
Impoliteness (rudeness)	ari	N	Individualistic (independent)	aqu	A
Imposing (dignified)	leo	A	Indoctrination (instruction)	vir	N
Imposition (pressuring)	ari	N	Industrious (hard-working)	cap	A
Imprecise (inexact)	sag	A	Ineptness (lacking skill)	tau	N
Impudence (effrontery)	aqu	N	Inequality (unfairness)	lib	N

Inexcusable (unjustifiable)	psc	A	Integrated (nonsectarian)	aqu	A
Inferred (speculated)	sag	A	Integration (commingling)	aqu	N
Infidelity (breach of vows)	sco	N	Intelligent (brilliant)	gem	A
Inflexibility (rigidity)	tau	N	Intense (consuming)	sco	A
Inflexible (unyielding)	tau	A	Intensity (pushiness)	ari	N
Influences (controls)	sco	A	Intention (purpose)	cap	N
Informal (casual)	sag	A	Intercedes (mediates)	lib	A
Informality (naturalness)	sag	N	Intercession (intervention)	lib	N
Information (message)	gem	N	Intermission (breather)	tau	N
Informed about (knows about)	gem	A	Internal (inward)	can	A
Ingesting (eating)	can	A	Interposed (among)	lib	A
Initiative (drive)	cap	N	Interpretation (clarification)	gem	N
Innocence (purity)	vir	N	Interpretation (explanation)	sco	N
Innocent (blameless)	tau	A	Intestinal (abdominal)	vir	A
Innocent (virtuous)	vir	A	Intimacy (close association)	leo	N
Inquiry (investigation)	sco	N	Intrigue (mystery)	sco	N
Inquisitive (curious)	gem	A	Introduces (makes known)	ari	A
Inquisitiveness (curiosity)	gem	N	Introduction (familiarization)	ari	N
Insecurity (self-doubt)	psc	N	Introductory (lead off)	ari	A
Insensitive (uncaring)	aqu	A	Invented (fabricated)	sag	A
Insensitivity (callousness)	aqu	N	Inverse (transposed)	lib	A
Insides (inner parts)	can	N	Inversion (reversal)	lib	N
Insincere (phony)	leo	A	Investigation (probing)	sco	N
Insincerity (phoniness)	leo	N	Invitation (summoning)	aqu	N
Insistent (emphatic)	ari	A	Invites (summons)	aqu	A
Instructions (guidelines)	cap	N	Inward (interior)	can	A
Insubordination (disobedience)	aqu	N	Irreligious (irreverent)	sco	A
			Irreverence (indifference)	aqu	N

Irrigation (wetting)	can	N	Leery (distrustful)	sco	A
Irritability (testiness)	can	N	Legality (legitimacy)	lib	N
Isolated (secluded)	psc	A	Legendary (fabled)	sag	A
Itemizes (lists)	vir	A	Legible (clear)	gem	A
Joint (shared)	lib	A	Legislative (lawmaking)	aqu	A
Jumping (leaping)	sag	N	Leisure Time (relaxation)	tau	N
Justification (rationalization)	sag	N	Leisurely (sluggish)	tau	A
Keeping (saving)	can	A	Leniency (mercy)	psc	N
Knowable (learnable)	gem	A	Lenient (merciful)	psc	A
Laborious (strenuous)	cap	A	Lethargic (sluggish)	tau	A
Land (one's nation)	can	N	Liable (answerable)	cap	A
Land (your property)	can	N	Liable (at fault)	lib	A
Large (big in size)	tau	A	Liberal (idealistic)	sag	A
Largeness (bigness)	tau	N	Liberation (freeing)	psc	N
Lattice (woven work)	can	N	License (permission)	sco	N
Latticed (grilled)	can	A	Lightness (paleness)	lib	N
Lavishness (extravagance)	leo	N	Like-Minded (agreeing)	lib	A
Lawmaking (political)	aqu	A	Likeness (sameness)	lib	N
Laziness (idleness)	leo	N	Limp (unstiff)	tau	A
Lazy (slow-moving)	tau	A	Lingering (unhurried)	tau	A
Leakproof (impervious)	can	A	Listlessness (weariness)	tau	N
Leakproof (watertight)	can	N	Literate (well-versed)	gem	A
Leaping (vaulting)	sag	N	Liturgical (ceremonial)	sag	A
Learnable (knowable)	gem	A	Livelihood (occupation)	cap	N
Learned (academic)	sag	A	Local (near)	gem	A
Learning (studying)	gem	N	Local (provincial)	can	A
Leathery (like leather)	cap	A	Logic (reasoning)	gem	N
Leave-Taking (departing)	sag	A	Lonely (friendless)	psc	A

Lonesome (unwanted)	psc	N	Meagerness (stinginess)	cap	N
Long-Winded (verbose)	sag	A	Measuring (marking out)	vir	N
Long-Windedness (verbosity)	sag	N	Mediates (arbitrates)	lib	A
Loose (slack)	tau	A	Mediation (arbitration)	lib	N
Lordly (boastful)	leo	A	Medical Interests (healing therapies)	vir	N
Loving (affectionate)	leo	A			
Loyal (faithful)	psc	A	Medicinal (hygienic)	vir	A
Loyalty (faithfulness)	psc	N	Meets (greets)	ari	A
Lumpy (uneven)	leo	A	Melodrama (sentimental drama)	can	N
Magic (sorcery)	sco	N			
Maintaining (keeping)	can	A	Melodramatic (emotional)	can	A
Making Ready (preparation)	cap	N	Membership (company)	aqu	N
Manageable (teachable)	cap	A	Mementos (keepsakes)	can	N
Management (administration)	cap	N	Memorable (notable)	can	A
Managing (administering)	cap	A	Memorial (monument)	can	N
Mannerly (polite)	lib	A	Memories (reminders)	can	N
Marital (conjugal)	lib	A	Mentioning (discussing)	gem	A
Marriage (merger)	lib	N	Merciful (forgiving)	psc	A
Marshy (watery)	can	A	Mercy (leniency)	psc	N
Massive (bulky)	tau	N	Method (process)	vir	N
Massive (gigantic)	tau	A	Meticulous (exacting)	vir	A
Matched (paired)	lib	A	Meticulous (thorough)	cap	A
Matched (uniformity)	lib	N	Mimicking (copying)	gem	A
Material (matter or stuff)	tau	N	Miniature (small)	tau	A
Material (tangible)	tau	A	Ministerial (ecclesiastical)	sag	A
Materialism (focus on values)	tau	N	Minor (petty)	vir	A
Materialistic (goods oriented)	tau	A	Mint (unused)	ari	A
Matter (material)	tau	N	Misconception (misjudgment)	lib	N

Overall Alphabetical List

Mismatched (unsuited)	lib	A	Naked (exposed)	ari	A
Mistrust (skepticism)	sco	N	Nakedness (barrenness)	ari	N
Mitigating (alleviating)	psc	A	Names (designates)	ari	A
Mitigation (alleviation)	psc	N	Narrates (explains)	gem	A
Mixes (combines)	aqu	A	Native (indigenous)	can	A
Mixture (blend)	aqu	N	Nattiness (style)	leo	N
Moderation (temperance)	tau	N	Natural (spontaneous)	leo	A
Modern (contemporary)	aqu	A	Natural (unadulterated)	tau	N
Modernization (updating)	aqu	N	Naturalness (spontaneity)	leo	N
Modest (proper)	vir	A	Nearby (close by)	gem	A
Modesty (decentness)	vir	N	Nearest (closest)	can	A
Modification (revision)	vir	N	Nearness (proximity)	gem	N
Money-Minded (prosperity seeking)	tau	A	Neat (tidy)	vir	A
			Neatness (orderliness)	vir	N
Moodiness (emotional feelings)	can	N	Negotiation (arbitration)	lib	N
			Neighborhood (area)	can	N
Moody (fickle)	can	A	Neighborly (friendly)	aqu	A
Motioning (signaling)	gem	A	Netlike (meshed)	can	A
Motionless (inactive)	tau	A	Networking (seeking cooperation)	aqu	N
Motive (reason)	ari	N			
Movement (activity)	ari	N	Neutral (colorless)	lib	A
Moving Forward (advancing)	ari	A	Neutrality (impartiality)	lib	N
Moving Upwards (ascending)	cap	N	Never (not ever)	sco	A
Multi-Hued (multi-colored)	lib	A	New (pristine)	ari	A
Municipal (civic)	aqu	A	New Age Ideas (open to the novel)	aqu	N
Mutual (joint)	lib	A			
Myth (legend)	sag	N	Next (subsequent)	tau	A
Mythical (legendary)	sag	A	Nimbleness (agility)	gem	N

Noble (distinguished)	leo	A	Obsession (absorption)	sco	N
Nonconformist (individualist)	aqu	N	Obstinacy (stubbornness)	tau	N
Nonpartisan (impartial)	lib	A	Obstinate (inflexible)	tau	A
Nostalgia (remembering)	can	N	Obtuse (dull witted)	tau	A
Nostalgic (sentimental)	can	A	Occult (the supernatural)	sco	N
Notable (remarkable)	leo	A	Occult Science (astrology)	aqu	N
Notch (mark)	can	N	Occupancy (tenancy)	can	N
Notched (toothed)	can	A	Occupation (business)	cap	N
Noteworthy (memorable)	can	A	Occupied (busy)	cap	A
Notices (sees)	gem	A	Off-the-Mark (imprecise)	sag	A
Nourishment (foodstuffs)	vir	N	Official (authorized)	cap	A
Nourishment (sustenance)	can	N	Offspring (issue)	leo	N
Novel (new)	aqu	A	Oneness (sameness)	lib	N
Nuptial (wedding)	lib	A	Open (accessible)	aqu	A
Nurturing (giving protection)	can	N	Opinion (point of view)	sag	N
Nurturing (mothering)	can	A	Opinionated (close-minded)	ari	A
Nutrition (good eating habits)	vir	N	Opposed (contradicting)	lib	A
Nutritious (nourishing)	vir	A	Opposite (inverse)	lib	N
Obedience (compliance)	vir	N	Oppresses (subjugates)	sco	A
Objection (complaint)	lib	N	Option (alternative)	lib	N
Objective (impartial)	aqu	A	Orderliness (uniformity)	vir	N
Obligated (duty bound)	sco	A	Orderly (arranged)	vir	A
Obligation (pledge)	sco	N	Orderly (regular)	cap	A
Obligation (responsibility)	cap	N	Organic (natural)	tau	N
Obliging (agreeable)	psc	A	Organization (system or arrangement)	vir	N
Observance (noticing)	gem	N			
Observes (notices)	gem	A	Organized (standardized)	cap	A
Obsessed with (controlled by)	sco	A	Organizes (classifies)	vir	A

Original (independent)	aqu	A	Parliamentary (legislative)	aqu	A
Ornate (elaborate)	leo	A	Part of (component)	vir	A
Orthodox (conventional)	tau	A	Particular (picky)	vir	N
Ostentation (display)	leo	N	Partnership (teaming)	lib	N
Outer Shell (covering)	can	N	Passion (emotion)	leo	N
Outreach (altruism)	aqu	N	Passive (tranquil)	tau	A
Outside (exterior)	can	A	Passive (yielding)	psc	A
Outspoken (forthright)	sag	A	Patience (composure)	tau	N
Overlay (overlap)	can	N	Patient (long-suffering)	tau	A
Overlooking (avoiding)	psc	N	Patriotic (nationalistic)	can	A
Oversensitive (impressionable)	psc	A	Patriotism (nationalism)	can	N
			Patronizing (condescending)	leo	A
Overstatement (embellishment)	sag	N	Paunchy (fatty)	tau	A
			Peace (harmony)	lib	N
Overview (broad picture)	sag	N	Penance (atonement)	psc	N
Ownership (possession)	can	N	Penetrating (incisive)	sco	A
Pagan (atheistic)	sco	A	Perfection (precision)	vir	N
Paired (coupled)	gem	A	Performance (execution)	cap	N
Paired (matched)	lib	A	Perfunctory (rushed through)	sag	A
Pale (washed out)	lib	A	Peripheral (outside)	can	A
Paleness (wanness)	lib	N	Permission (consent)	sco	N
Panoramic (sweeping)	sag	A	Permits (allows)	sco	A
Parallel (side-by-side)	lib	A	Persistence (determination)	cap	N
Pardoning (forgiving)	psc	A	Persistent (tenacious)	cap	A
Parentage (ancestry)	can	N	Perspective (big picture)	sag	N
Parental (maternal or paternal)	can	A	Pertinent (germane)	cap	A
Parenting (raising offspring)	can	N	Perverted (kinky)	sco	A
Parity (equality)	lib	N	Petty (trivial)	vir	A

Philosophical (envisioned)	sag	A	Possession (holding or tenure)	can	N
Phoniness (insincerity)	leo	N	Possessive (acquisitive)	can	A
Phony (insincere)	leo	A	Possible (attainable)	cap	A
Picky (fussy)	vir	N	Possible (likely)	sag	A
Piece (component or morsel)	can	N	Powder (dust or fine grains)	can	N
Piece (component)	vir	N	Powdery (granulated)	can	A
Pit (dent or groove)	can	N	Practical (realistic)	tau	A
Pitiless (hard-hearted)	cap	A	Practical (useful)	cap	A
Pitted (pock marked)	can	A	Practicality (usefulness)	tau	N
Pitying (sympathizing)	psc	A	Practices (trains)	vir	A
Placating (appeasing)	psc	A	Pragmatism (practicality)	tau	N
Plan (objective)	cap	N	Praise (acclaim)	leo	N
Planning (scheduling)	cap	N	Praising (flattering)	leo	A
Plans for (schedules)	cap	A	Precaution (safeguard)	can	N
Playful (frolicsome)	leo	A	Precise (explicit)	vir	A
Pledge (promise)	sco	N	Precision (accuracy)	vir	N
Pliable (flexible)	gem	A	Precursor (forerunner)	ari	N
Pointed Objects	sag	N	Preferred (favored)	lib	A
(e.g., needles, scissors)			Preliminary (at the beginning)	ari	A
Poise (composure)	lib	N	Premise (assumption)	sag	N
Poised (dignified)	lib	A	Preoccupation (daydreaming)	sag	N
Political (civil)	aqu	A	Preoccupied (absorbed with)	sco	A
Pompous (high-sounding)	leo	A	Preparation (plan)	cap	N
Popularity (recognition)	leo	N	Prepared (cooked)	vir	A
Portion (part or piece)	vir	N	Prepared (ready)	cap	A
Position	cap	N	Preservation (saving)	can	N
(function or occupation)			Preserving (conserving)	can	A
Positive (emphatic)	ari	A	Presumed (approximated)	sag	A

Presumptuous (arrogant)	ari	A	Proud (self-contented)	leo	A
Pretended (assumed)	leo	A	Proverb (adage)	sag	N
Pretense (pretending)	leo	N	Provincial (regional)	can	A
Prevails (determined)	cap	A	Provisions (supplies)	vir	N
Preview (advance showing)	ari	N	Pulling Together (teamwork)	lib	N
Pride (self-importance)	leo	N	Purchases (obtains)	can	A
Principled (law-abiding)	cap	A	Pure (unmarked or clean)	lib	A
Pristine (unused)	lib	A	Purity (sanitizing)	lib	N
Privacy (secrecy)	sco	N	Purpose (reason)	ari	N
Private (nonpublic)	sco	A	Purposeful (deliberate)	sco	A
Procedure (individual steps)	vir	N	Puzzling (baffling)	sco	A
Proceeding (moving ahead)	ari	A	Qualifications (certification)	cap	N
Productive (fruitful)	tau	A	Qualified (eligible)	cap	A
Productive (useful)	cap	A	Questioning (asking)	gem	A
Proficiency (know-how)	gem	N	Questioning (curiosity)	gem	N
Progressive (trend-setting)	aqu	A	Quiet (still)	tau	A
Prominence (conspicuousness)	leo	N	Rambling (discursive)	sag	A
Prompt (on time)	cap	A	Ramblings (digressions)	sag	N
Proper (ethical)	cap	A	Rashness (franticness)	ari	N
Proper (formal)	vir	A	Reachable (attainable)	cap	A
Proper (suitable)	lib	A	Readiness (preparedness)	cap	N
Proportionate (equivalent)	lib	A	Ready (prepared)	cap	A
Prosperous (flourishing)	tau	A	Real (actual)	tau	A
Protected (preserved)	sco	A	Realistic (practical)	tau	A
Protection (safe conduct)	can	N	Reality (actuality)	tau	N
Protective (shielding)	can	A	Reason (grounds)	ari	N
Protruding (showing)	leo	A	Reasoning (thinking through)	gem	A
Protrusion (projection)	leo	N	Reasoning	gem	N

(working things out)			Relaxation (taking it easy)	tau	N
Rebellion (insurrection)	aqu	N	Relaxed (laid-back)	tau	A
Rebuke (censure or scolding)	sco	N	Release (letting go)	psc	N
Receptivity to the New	aqu	N	Releasing (freeing)	psc	A
Reciprocates (retaliates)	sco	A	Relevance (aptness)	lib	N
Reciprocity (interplay)	sco	N	Reliability (responsibility)	cap	N
Reckless (foolhardy)	ari	A	Reliable (dependable)	tau	A
Recklessness (heedlessness)	ari	N	Reliable (loyal)	psc	A
Reclusive (withdrawn)	psc	A	Reliable (trusty)	cap	A
Reclusiveness (withdrawal)	psc	N	Reliance (confidence)	cap	N
Records (documents)	gem	A	Reliance (dependence)	can	N
Recreation (entertainment)	leo	N	Relief (comfort)	psc	N
Redundancy (duplication)	gem	N	Relieving (soothing)	psc	A
Redundant (repetitive)	gem	A	Religious (holy)	vir	A
Refined (cultivated)	lib	A	Religious (theological)	sag	A
Refinement (tastefulness)	lib	N	Reluctant (hesitant)	cap	A
Reflection (mirroring)	gem	N	Remedial (curing)	vir	N
Refrains from (avoids)	sco	A	Remembering (not forgetting)	can	A
Regional (provincial)	can	A	Reminders (mementos)	can	N
Regular (uniform or orderly)	cap	A	Remote (distant)	sag	A
Regularity (consistency)	tau	N	Removed (aloof)	aqu	A
Regulates (controls)	sco	A	Renounces (repudiates)	sco	A
Regulation (administration)	cap	N	Renunciation (abdication)	psc	N
Regulations (rules)	sco	N	Reparation	psc	N
Rejects (declines)	sco	A	(redress or amends)		
Rejects (spurns)	psc	A	Repayment	sco	N
Related (similar)	gem	A	(redress or amends)		
Relative (coequal)	lib	A	Replica (likeness)	gem	N

Represses (shuts in)	sco	A	Rigidity (firmness)	tau	N
Reprimand (berating)	sco	N	Ritual (ceremony)	vir	N
Reprimands (scolds)	sco	A	Rivalry (competitiveness)	lib	N
Reptilian (leathery)	cap	A	Rotates (switches)	aqu	A
Requires (obligates)	sco	A	Rough (guessed at)	sag	A
Research (investigation)	sco	N	Rough Idea (overview)	sag	N
Resemblance (similarity)	gem	N	Roundabout (indirect)	sag	A
Resentment (mistrust)	sco	N	Rudeness (impoliteness)	ari	N
Reserved (indifferent)	aqu	A	Rule (criterion)	sco	N
Reserved (withdrawn)	cap	A	Rural (country)	can	A
Residential (domestic)	can	A	Rural Practices (agriculture)	can	N
Resoluteness (resolve)	cap	N	Rushing (speeding)	ari	A
Respite (letup)	psc	N			
Responsibility (accountability)	cap	N	Rustic (rural)	can	A
			Sacrifice (self-denial)	psc	N
Responsible (answerable)	cap	A	Sacrifice (yielding)	psc	N
Resting (relaxing)	tau	A	Safeguarding (protecting)	can	N
Restitution (repayment)	sco	N	Safekeeping (having responsibility)	can	N
Restraint (self-control)	tau	N			
Restricted (confined)	psc	A	Safety (keeping watchfulness)	can	N
Restriction (confinement)	psc	N	Saintly (pious)	vir	A
Retaliation (retribution)	sco	N	Sanctioned (authorized)	cap	A
Revealing (disclosing)	gem	A	Sanctions (confirms)	sco	A
Revenge (vindication)	sco	N	Satisfaction (gratification)	tau	N
Revengeful (vindictive)	sco	A	Saturation (wetness)	can	N
Reversal (transposition)	lib	N	Saving (collecting)	can	N
Reverse (inverse)	lib	A	Scales (laminar coating)	can	N
Review (second look)	vir	N	Scaly (flaky)	can	A
Rightfulness (legality)	lib	N	Scatters (strews)	aqu	A

Schedules (prepares)	cap	A	Sensible (prudent)	cap	A
Scheme (stratagem)	sag	N	Sensible (rational)	tau	A
Scholarly (academic)	gem	A	Sensitive (susceptible)	psc	A
Schooled (instructed)	gem	A	Sensitivity (impressionability)	psc	N
Schooled (learned)	sag	A	Sensuality (carnality)	tau	N
Schooling (learning)	gem	N	Sentiment	can	N
Scolding (reprimand)	sco	N	(feelings or attitude)		
Scolds (chides)	sco	A	Sentimental (emotional)	can	A
Scrambles (mixes)	aqu	A	Separation (breaking-up)	lib	N
Scrutiny (examination)	vir	N	Sequence (order)	vir	N
Sealed (watertight)	can	N	Serene (calm)	tau	A
Seclusion (isolation)	psc	N	Serenity (tranquility)	tau	N
Secrecy (privacy)	sco	N	Service (help or assistance)	vir	N
Secretive (hidden)	sco	A	Settles (resolves)	lib	A
Secures (attaches)	can	A	Shaggy (fuzzy)	can	A
Securing (fastening)	can	N	Shared (divided)	lib	A
Sees (observes)	gem	A	Sharing (participation)	aqu	N
Segment (portion)	vir	A	Shelter (housing)	can	N
Select (exclusive)	lib	A	Shielding (protective)	can	A
Selective (fastidious)	vir	A	Shifts (switches)	aqu	A
Self-Centered (conceited)	ari	A	Shirking (evading)	psc	N
Self-Centeredness	ari	N	Shortcoming (drawback)	psc	N
(focus on self)			Shrouded (cloaked)	psc	A
Self-Control (restraint)	tau	N	Shunned (disregarded)	psc	A
Self-Doubt (insecurity)	psc	N	Shut-In (confined)	psc	A
Self-Oriented (egotistical)	ari	A	Shy (bashful)	psc	A
Selfish (self-centered)	ari	A	Shyness (modesty)	vir	N
Sensations (perceptions)	tau	N	Sick (in poor health)	vir	A

Sidewise (indirect)	can	A	Socialization (mingling)	aqu	N
Sidewise Motion (indirectness)	can	N	Society (community)	aqu	N
Signal (communication)	gem	N	Soft-Hearted (merciful)	psc	A
Similar (alike)	gem	A	Sogginess (wetness)	can	N
Similarity (resemblance)	gem	N	Soggy (waterlogged)	can	A
Simple (uninvolved)	tau	A	Solace (consolation)	psc	N
Simultaneous (concurrent)	lib	A	Solemn (ceremonial)	vir	A
Sincerity (earnestness)	sag	N	Solicitation (asking)	psc	N
Single-Mindedness (fixation)	sco	N	Soliciting (begging)	psc	A
Skeptical (doubting)	sco	A	Solid (firm)	tau	A
Skepticism (doubt)	sco	N	Solidity (denseness)	tau	N
Skilled (proficient)	cap	A	Solitary (by oneself)	psc	A
Skillfulness (handiness)	gem	N	Solitude (seclusion)	psc	N
Slack (drooping)	tau	A	Soon (impending)	tau	A
Slight (small)	tau	A	Sophistication (worldliness)	leo	N
Slimy (viscous)	can	A	Sorcery (witchcraft)	sco	N
Slow (unhurried)	tau	A	Source (basis)	can	N
Slowness (simple-mindedness)	tau	N	Spared (exempted)	sco	A
Sly (devious)	sco	A	Speckled (spotted)	lib	A
Small (little or tiny)	tau	A	Speculative (hypothetical)	sag	A
Smart (intelligent)	gem	A	Spiteful (revengeful)	sco	A
Smell (odor)	ari	N	Spontaneity (naturalness)	leo	N
Smelly (ill-smelling)	ari	A	Spontaneous (extemporaneous)	leo	A
Smug (complacent)	leo	A			
Sneaky (secretive)	sco	A	Spotted (mottled)	lib	A
Social Behavior (propriety)	lib	N	Stability (firmness)	tau	N
Social Interaction (social engagement)	lib	N	Stabilization (equilibrium)	lib	N
			Stable (firm or steady)	tau	A

Stamina (endurance)	tau	N	Sturdiness (solidness)	tau	N
Standards (criteria)	cap	N	Stylish (classy or high-toned)	leo	A
Standards (instructions)	cap	N	Stylishness (popular mannerism)	leo	N
Stands Apart (separate from)	aqu	A			
Start (first step)	ari	N	Subject to (dependent on)	can	A
Starting (beginning)	ari	A	Submission (yielding)	psc	N
Steadiness (reliability)	tau	N	Submissive (yielding)	psc	A
Stealth (secrecy)	sco	N	Subsistence (provisions)	can	N
Sterile (clean)	vir	A	Substance (material or stuff)	tau	N
Sterilization (disinfection)	vir	N	Substantial (bulky or heavy)	tau	A
Stern (strict or demanding)	cap	A	Suggestibility (receptiveness)	psc	N
Sticking (holding)	can	N	Suitability (aptness)	cap	N
Sticky (gummy or tacky)	can	A	Suitability (relevance)	lib	N
Still (unmoving)	tau	A	Suitable (appropriate)	cap	A
Stinginess (cheapness)	cap	N	Summoning (bringing together)	aqu	N
Stocks (furnishes)	vir	A			
Strenuous (laborious)	cap	A	Summons (invites)	aqu	A
Stretched (enhanced)	sag	A	Supernatural (the occult)	sco	N
Strews (throws around)	aqu	A	Supervision (oversight)	cap	N
Strict (merciless)	cap	A	Supplies (equips)	vir	A
Stronghold (fortification)	can	N	Supporter (backer)	aqu	N
Stubborn (obstinate)	tau	A	Supportive (helpful)	vir	A
Stubbornness (willfulness)	tau	N	Suppresses (restrains)	sco	A
Stuck-up (pompous)	leo	A	Susceptibility (sensitiveness)	psc	N
Study (investigation)	sco	N	Susceptible (trusting)	psc	A
Study (learning)	gem	N	Suspicion (doubt)	sco	N
Stunt (feat or trick)	sag	N	Suspicious (mistrustful)	sco	A
Stupidity (empty headedness)	tau	N	Sustaining (prolonging)	tau	A

Sweat (perspiration)	ari	N	Theatrics (showmanship)	leo	N
Sweeping (broad or extensive)	sag	A	Theoretical (speculative)	sag	A
Swelling (bulge)	leo	N	Theory (hypothesis)	sag	N
Switches (varies)	aqu	A	Thinking (brainwork)	gem	N
Swollen (distended)	leo	A	Thinking (deliberating)	gem	A
Symbol (metaphor)	sag	N	Thirsty (dehydrated)	ari	A
Symmetrical (proportional)	lib	A	Thorough (conscientious)	cap	A
Symmetry (uniformity)	lib	N	Thorough (particular)	sco	A
Sympathetic (compassionate)	psc	A	Thoughtless (indiscreet)	ari	A
Sympathy (compassion)	psc	N	Thrifty (frugal)	cap	A
Synchronized (in agreement)	lib	A	Thriving (flourishing)	tau	N
Systematic (methodical)	cap	A	Throng (crowd)	aqu	N
Tactic (plot or strategy)	sag	N	Thrown Together (slapdash)	sag	A
Talk (discussion)	gem	N	Tidy (neat or orderly)	vir	A
Talkative (gabby)	gem	A	Tight-Fistedness (stinginess)	cap	N
Talking (jabberer)	gem	N	Tightness (packed in)	aqu	N
Teamwork (cooperation)	lib	N	Timid (bashful)	psc	A
Teamwork (pulling together)	aqu	N	Timidity (cowardice)	leo	N
Technical (methodical)	cap	A	Together (in unison)	lib	A
Technique	vir	N	Toilsome (laborious)	cap	A
(procedure or routine)			Tolerance (lenience)	psc	N
Teeming (filled)	aqu	A	Tolerant (humanitarian)	aqu	A
Temperance (moderation)	tau	N	Tolerant (passive)	psc	A
Tenacity (persistence)	cap	N	Tolerant (patient)	tau	A
Tenancy (occupation)	can	N	Toleration (forbearance)	tau	N
Territory (area or region)	can	N	Toothed (serrated)	can	A
Tested (tried)	cap	A	Touchable (tangible)	tau	A
Thatch (hair)	can	N	Touching (caressing)	can	A

Traditional (customary)	can	A	Undertaking (project)	cap	N
Training (practice or drill)	vir	N	Uneasiness (disquiet)	vir	N
Trains (practices)	vir	A	Unethical (immoral)	sco	A
Tranquility (calm or quiet)	tau	N	Unfaithful (disloyal)	sco	A
Transparency (clearness)	lib	N	Unfeeling (callous)	aqu	A
Transparent (clear or see-through)	lib	A	Unfettered (freedom loving)	sag	N
			Unforced (natural)	leo	A
Transposed (inverted)	lib	A	Ungainly (awkward)	tau	A
Treachery (betrayal)	sco	N	Unhampered (unobstructed)	sag	A
Trendsetting (modernization)	aqu	N	Unhurried (leisurely)	tau	A
Trivial (trifling)	vir	A	Uniform (consistent)	cap	A
Trusting (susceptible)	psc	A	Uniformity (consistency)	tau	N
Tutors (trains)	vir	A	Unimaginative (boring)	tau	A
Twin (doubled)	gem	A	Unintentional (inadvertent)	sag	A
Tyrannical (dictatorial)	sco	A	Unique (distinct)	aqu	A
Unambiguity (clarity)	lib	N	Uniqueness (distinguishment)	aqu	N
Unambiguous (explicit)	vir	A	United (together)	lib	A
Unarranged (thrown together)	sag	A	Unknowable (baffling)	sco	A
Unblocked (unobstructed)	sag	A	Unmarked (unblemished)	lib	A
Unchanging (unwavering)	tau	N	Unmarked (undefaced)	vir	A
Unclaimed (abandoned)	psc	A	Unobstructed (clear)	sag	A
Uncommitted (unplanned)	sag	A	Unpointed (pointless)	tau	A
Uncomplicated (simple)	tau	A	Unprotected (unguarded)	can	A
Unconcern (indifference)	aqu	N	Unresponsive (reserved)	cap	A
Unconcerned (uninterested)	aqu	A	Unscheduled (unintended)	sag	A
Undecided (vacillating)	lib	A	Unsharp (dull)	tau	A
Undefended (defenseless)	can	A	Unskillful (inept)	tau	N
Understandable (lucid)	gem	A	Unsuited (mismatched)	lib	A

Unused (new)	ari	A	Warm (hospitable)	leo	A
Urgency (dire necessity)	ari	N	Warmth (affection)	leo	N
Useful (functional or helpful)	cap	A	Wary (cautious)	cap	A
Usefulness (functionality)	cap	N	Washed Out (blanched)	lib	A
Usefulness (serviceability)	tau	N	Watchfulness (alertness)	can	N
Uses (trains with)	vir	A	Watertight (impermeable)	can	A
Vacancy (emptiness or void)	ari	N	Watertight (leakproof)	can	N
Vacant (empty)	ari	A	Weaving (interlacing)	can	N
Vacillation (ambivalence)	lib	N	Weighing (considering)	lib	N
Vague (ambiguous)	psc	A	Welfare (allotment)	psc	N
Vagueness (generality)	sag	N	Well-Versed (scholarly)	sag	A
Vain (proud)	leo	A	Wetness (sogginess)	can	N
Validity (soundness)	cap	N	Whining (complaining)	vir	A
Vanity (egotism)	leo	N	White (colorless)	lib	A
Variation (diversity)	aqu	N	Widespread (extended)	sag	A
Verbose (wordy)	sag	A	Willful (deliberate)	sco	A
Verbosity (wordiness)	sag	N	Wise to (informed about)	gem	A
Verifiable (determinable)	gem	A	Withdrawal (secession)	psc	N
Verifies (substantiates)	sco	A	Withdrawn (distant)	cap	A
Vindication (justification)	sco	N	Wool (fleece or fuzz)	can	N
Vindictive (vengeful)	sco	A	Woolly (fleecy)	can	A
Virginity (chastity)	vir	N	Working (operative)	cap	A
Virtue (decency)	vir	N	Worry (anxiety)	vir	N
Virtuous (chaste)	vir	A	Woven (interlaced)	can	A
Vocal (spoken)	gem	A	Yielding (compliant)	psc	A
Vulnerable (insecure)	can	A	Zealous (excited)	ari	A
Wandering (roaming)	psc	A	Zigzagged (serrated)	can	A
Wanderlust (need to roam)	sag	N			

Also by Michael Munkasey:

American Federation of Astrologers, Inc

References and Sources

• The Synonym Finder, J. I. Rodale, 1978 Rodale Press

• Merriam-Webster's Collegiate Dictionary, 11th Edition, 2008, Merriam-Webster Incorporated

• House Keywords and More … ; Michael Munkasey; 2018; American Federation of Astrologers, Tempe, AZ, USA

• Midpoints: Unleashing the Power of the Planets; Michael Munkasey; 2018; ACS Publications, New Hampshire, USA

• Article: Astrological Symbols and Keywords; Michael Munkasey; NCGR Research Journal, Vol. 4, Spring 2014

www.ingramcontent.com/pod-product-compliance
Lightning Source LLC
Chambersburg PA
CBHW081616170426
43195CB00041B/2855